COLLEGE STUDENTS:
DO THIS!
GET HIRED!

D1507393

From Freshman to Ph.D.
The secrets, tips, techniques and tricks you need to
get the Full Time Job, Co-Op, or Summer Internship
position you want

by Mark Lyden
A Professional Fortune 500
College Recruiter

www.DoThisGetHired.com

Contents

CHAPTER 5:

I teach you one easy to remember method that really works. I walk you through it step-by-step. Also, I give you 3 Crazy Good Tips and tell you the most effective way to follow up.

CHAPTER 6:

If you don't follow this advice, you probably won't get hired because chances are you won't even be considered. I give you 7 steps to follow that will give you a significant competitive advantage

CHAPTER 7:

I show you exactly how you do it and teach you a technique that will maximize your chances at getting more money.

CHAPTER 8:

How to do it and what you really can get out of it. This is more important than you might think.

CHAPTER 9:

Assorted advice to help you put your best foot forward. Also included is specific advice for each year of college.

Acknowledgements

Dr. Richard Sanzenbacher: Thank you for all the great advice, support, and editing of this book. You have been very generous with your time. I continue to use the skills you taught me in your classes. I believe these skills have greatly contributed to my professional success as well as my success in life.

Dr. Neil Campbell: Thank you for being a great mentor and taking the time to see my potential. I appreciate you showing me the great fun behind recruiting and for your continued friendship and support throughout my career.

Mark C.: To a great mentor and friend. I appreciate you always listening. I know you have kept me out of trouble a time or two with your sage advice. Thanks for always supporting my career and ideas. Thank you for helping motivate me to write this book. I have learned a lot from you.

Andrew G.: Thank you for your great enthusiasm for life, your willingness to always go the extra mile, and for your great, infectious, positive attitude. I know I speak for many when I say thanks for seeing and acknowledging the hard work and extra efforts of the people around you.

To my Family and Friends: For your kind words and support not only with this book, but also throughout my life.

INTRODUCTION

What Qualifies Me to Give You Advice

What my experience is so you can decide for yourself the value of my advice.

I'm not going to waste your time. I am not going to simply regurgitate points from other books in a different format. Make no mistake: This book will be *different* because it teaches you how to get a college level full-time job, co-op, or summer internship from a *current, experienced, college Recruiter's* point of view. However, I think it is important to start by letting you know just what my experience is so you can decide the value of the following information:

- I have been a lead college recruiter for a Fortune 500 company now for over 10 years
- In my professional college recruiting career, I have recruited for small, medium, and large-sized companies
- I have interviewed and screened thousands of candidates

> *Who better to teach you how to get the job you want, than the person who evaluates college students for a living; an experienced College recruiter!*

- I have created seminars and presented to approximately 10,000 students on college campuses and recruiting events from coast to coast
- I have designed and taught classes on the secrets, tips, techniques, tricks, and the inside story behind Resume

Writing, Interviewing, Career Fair, Negotiating Salary, Applying Online, How To Be a Great Intern, How to be Successful at Your First Job, etc…

- I have mentored hundreds of employees, co-ops, interns, and prospective candidates
- I led or participated in well over 100 different career fairs and expos across the country
- I have led many minority recruiting events at Historically Black Colleges and Universities (HBCUs) as well as Minority Institutions (MI)
- I have led or participated in recruiting at national conventions and symposiums along with national, regional, and local recruiting events affiliated with dozens and dozens of student groups including but not limited to NSBE, SHPE, SWE, MBAs, AIAA, IEEE, Golden Key, and many, many more
- I recruited for the majority of technical and non-technical majors out there at all levels from Freshman through Ph.D.
- I have recruited for Secret and Top Secret programs
- I have been responsible for negotiating candidate salaries
- I have hired or helped in the process of hiring thousands of candidates from Freshman to Ph.D. levels
- I trained, advised, and mentored well over 100 different people on how to recruit great people and the techniques to do so. I have taught engineers, business people, executives, new hires and even interns on recruiting methods and processes
- I have managed all aspects of an intern / co-op program with hundreds of students per year, many of which had been selected by me. This program has been rated amongst the best in the nation
- I continue to do all these things, full time, as my profession

Now with that experience, knowledge, and success, I want to help you learn the inside story behind how college students get hired. Whether you're looking for a co-op, summer internship or full time job; whether you're a freshman or a Ph. D. student; whether your major is technical or non-technical, *what you will find in these pages will give* *you a **significant competitive advantage** in landing the career you **want**.*

Throughout the book, I have incorporated actual true stories about situations I have experienced that make a particular point. These stories include actual students just like you and in many ways are the best ways to illustrate an important point you need to know.

I could have probably written a separate book on each one of the major topics I have included in this one. I might do that in the future if the market supports it because there is a lot of things I have learned and discovered that I can pass on; things that can really help those currently in college, about to go to college, or been out of college for only a couple of years. But for now, I wanted to write a book that got to the point about each of the major job hunting areas included in the process of finding a summer internship, co-op, or full time position. In this book, you will find the best tips, tricks, secrets, and techniques I have seen work for students. Most of these techniques I have learned, created, or developed from my experience and work with past candidates. I have seen these techniques consistently work and work well; some of them being the critical step in helping students land the position they wanted in the company they wanted to work for.

> *Sure other books are longer and have hundreds of things for you to try, so do many websites, but I am just going to share with you what works best!*

I have read or reviewed many of the books and websites out there giving you advice on what you should do in your job search. This is one of the reasons why I decided to write this book. This advice is not always good and too many times it is just completely wrong. I know what works and what doesn't because I live it. I teach it. This is my career; my profession. I see the results of different techniques. I study and analyze what other company representatives are doing and saying. This is part of my job. I need to know what is happening out there each year, each semester so I can be successful and I can teach others how to be successful with recruiting the best candidates. Anyone telling you their way works all the time is lying. To put it another way, if one method worked all the time, then there wouldn't be a need for this book or any of the dozens out there. However, I am providing information on what I have seen consistently works, year after year.

Now I am not going to preach that everyone should come up with some huge elaborate plan with a time line that illustrates everything that needs to be done -- then tell you to hang it on your wall so you can visualize it every day...because most of you won't do that. So I am going to be as realistic as I can so you can benefit the most in the limited time we have together.

Definition of Job: Landing a summer internship or co-op is very similar to scoring a full time position. There are some differences that I will point out at the appropriate time but for now when I say a "job," I am referring to any position including co-op, summer intern, and full time.

STORY: So about a year ago, I was on a college campus recruiting and I had some time before my next meeting. I went into the library and noticed a small display of books as I entered. They were books that the librarian chose to display because they were all about finding a job, and it was right before the career fair on campus. I picked up a book by some Ph.D., opened to one section and started to read. I was surprised by what he was telling the reader. Yes, some points were correct, but others were totally off base and wrong from my experiences. Plus, it took him about ten pages in each chapter just to get to the point. Then, when he did, the point was incomplete. I read further and began to get irritated. Here was this Ph. D. who wrote this book to help college students and half of what he said was incomplete or downright wrong. I found myself saying "NO!" in my mind, and then out loud. Of course then I looked up to see if anyone heard me. A few did. The reason why there are so many "self help" books out there on how to get a job and the processes involved in getting a job is because it inherently is a soft science based a lot on opinion. These books have the standard topics like interviewing or resume writing and they tell you what they think. For example, what if you have a GPA that is a 2.9/4.0? Do you put it on your resume or do you leave it off? There are strong opinions and points on both sides. Many say, "If your GPA is not a 3.0 or higher, you should never put it on your resume." I think this is just dead wrong. Why? Let me give you an example. If hiring managers have ten, twenty, fifty, or two hundred resumes in front of them for one position, do you really think they are going to take the time to call or e-mail potential candidates to ask them what their GPA is because they didn't have it on their resume? I can tell you...they won't do it. Your resume goes into the "No" pile immediately and the game for you is over. Yes, they are probably disregarding some really great candidates. But remember, they have other things to do, and recruiting and reviewing resumes is not their full time job. For the most part hiring managers want to get the candidate count down to a manageable number and then move on from there. One of the easiest ways of getting the countdown to this manageable level is to simply count out all those without GPAs on their resume. Here is an analogy to clarify my point: Let's say you want to become a fighter pilot for the US Navy and one of the criteria is that you must have 20/20 vision. You have 20/25 vision. You are out. No questions asked. With this approach, there is an excellent chance that the Navy is counting out some outstanding future fighter pilots. However, they have plenty of candidates to pick from with 20/20 vision. There are many other reasons why you should have your GPA on your resume even if it is a little low. I cover many of them in Chapter 3, Resumes.

The danger in writing a book like this is that I have to give you the reader some background information about who college recruiters really are and how they operate. The first two chapters of this book do this. Those close to me say these two chapters are really good and have great information in them, but when compared to the powerful information in the rest of the chapters, they say they are not as exciting to read.

I get it. I agree. But this background information really helps bring together information you will learn and gives, in most cases, a greater understanding to why some technique, tip or trick works with college recruiters. Don't worry though both chapters are short. However, if you are one of those people that can't wait and just needs to get to the coolest stuff, skip to Chapter 3 and start from there. But then when you are done, come back and read the first two chapters so you get the full benefit of the book.

MY DEAL WITH YOU THE READER:

If I help you with the advice and information in these pages, the deal I would like to make with you is that you simply let me know. My e-mail address is Mark@DoThisGetHired.com. Plus, I want your feedback and would sincerely appreciate your review of the book. If you like something or don't like something in this book, drop me an e-mail. If you have a suggestion to make the book better in the future, please let me know. Remember, most of the techniques, tips, tricks and secrets you are going to read about were developed from my experiences with students just like you. I want to hear your thoughts and experiences dealing with what you have read in this book. If my advice helped you in a particular situation, please e-mail me with the details; perhaps I can use it in the future to help others. I might even publish it in my next book or on my website to help teach others how the advice might work for them. And, of course, if you have questions, you can e-mail me or go to my website, www.DoThisGetHired.com and check out the helpful information and FAQs I have there. I also have a lot of great links to help you as well.

Chapter 1

The Inside Story on College Recruiting

Those things you need to know that will really help you understand what college recruiters do and why we do it.

College recruiting is dynamic. As things change, such as technology, the economy, supply and demand of certain skills (to name a few), so does the approach to college recruiting from year to year and even semester to semester. College recruiters need to adapt to the changing times. Those that have been doing it for a while even have to change with new generations. However, there are also some things that stay the same even over the years and through all the changes. One such thing is recruiters trying to find the best candidates for the open jobs.

For those of you who are engineers or technical people, the process of recruiting candidates is not all a "hard" skill like a mathematical equation where you simply follow the steps and you get the right answer. There is a significant amount of "soft" skills like psychology, communication, etc. Ironically, when you are a candidate looking for a job, for you to put your best foot forward, there are simple equations you should follow which of course I will cover. The brightest minds in Human Resources (HR), Psychology, Talent Acquisition, to name a few, have tried everything to make recruiting more objective; to take the soft skills like opinions and feelings out of the process. But the fact still remains that no matter what has been done, no matter what methods or processes have been implemented, *there is still and will always be some subjectivity when evaluating people.* Those professionals, in the before mentioned fields, don't want to admit this, but they know it to be true. They resist admitting it simply because they are hired to take the subjectivity out of the recruiting process. Agreeing that this can't be done is like telling the companies they are employed by that they can't do their job. Plus, have you noticed that the majority of the recruiters behind the Career Fair booth seem to be HR types or non-technical people? Want to know why? Simple again. In general, they are better at the soft skills than the engineers and technical types. They are better at the subjective side of the recruiting equation. That being said, some of the very best recruiters I have ever worked with are engineers or technical people; however, they were able to learn both the objective and *subjective* side of recruiting and this is rare so there are very few out there.

> *To a college recruiter, your ATTITUDE is the most important attribute we look for. It is more important than GPA, Experience, Leadership, EVERYTHING!*

This makes perfect sense because if you don't know already, the vast majority of on-campus or initial candidate interviews are behavioral in nature. They are most commonly known as behavioral or structural interviews. Why is that? This is another great question with a simple answer. It is because the right *attitude* is the most important attribute you, the candidate must have. It trumps everything else. *Your attitude is the most critical item when being evaluated or interviewed.* It is not your grades. It is not how good you are as a team player. It is not your leadership skills. It is not even your intern, co-op or work experience. All very important things I admit, but not nearly as important as you having the right attitude.

To illustrate this point and take it one step further, here is a question for you the reader: What do you think is the biggest fear of a hiring manger is when hiring a college student? Some might say it is hiring someone that can't do the work. But that's not it. In my experience, hiring managers are most fearful of hiring someone with a bad attitude. Why? Because it often has a domino effect that can be very damaging. Hiring someone with a bad attitude negatively affects the whole team. That in turn causes conflict. Conflict lowers morale. Lowering morale increases inefficiency. Inefficiency translates into lost time and money....which is misery for guess who? The hiring manager! At least, if the hiring manager hires an employee that can't do the work, they have a fighting chance to work around it by sending them off for training or giving them different assignments; having them do work they can do. But having a college hire with a bad attitude is nothing short of throwing a psychological grenade in the middle of the room with all team members present.

Moreover, who do you think gets a lot of the blame, or even becomes the scapegoat if a college candidate gets hired that has a bad attitude? Yes, you are right; the college recruiter! So wouldn't it be logical for a company to send out those people that tend to be the best at screening for this relatively subjective, very soft science attribute we call attitude? That is why you see mostly HR and business type people out on campus doing the initial screening. Engineers and technical people tend to concentrate and be more comfortable evaluating attributes that they can quantify, like GPA, months of intern or co-op experience, or even leadership. But again, it is your attitude that is most important. The recruiter's mantra is, "hire for attitude, and train for skill."

Chapter 2

The Truth About College Recruiters

What you need to know about us and why knowing it is very important in the development of your approach when communicating with us.

Really, when you boil it down, college recruiters are just sales people. You, the candidate, sell yourself to us. We sell you back to managers, and sell you on the company. What I have leaned is there are good recruiters out there, but there are as many poor recruiters out there as good ones. Plus, there are very few great recruiters. You, the candidate, have no clue who is great, good, or poor. But you really don't need to know as long as you are prepared for the poor ones.

> *The experience level and training of the people that you see behind the career fair booth or the interview table fluctuates vastly!*

The poor recruiters are what I will prepare you for because if you can get through them, the good and great recruiters will think you are nothing but fantastic!

But what is your definition of a college recruiter? Many of the people you see behind the booth at a career fair, especially at large companies, are not recruiters at all. You have been programmed to think they are recruiters because, well, they are behind the career fair booth. However, in reality, most are "campus team members." That means, they don't recruit for a living and have other full time jobs with the company. Recruiting is something they may do once or maybe twice a year if that. A high percentage of the people you meet on campus calling themselves recruiters are not trained in recruiting at any significant level. Here is who they may be:

- First timers that are simply in training
- Hiring managers that go out once a year
- Human Resource people that may or may not have any recruiting experience (Often people assume that just because a person is in HR, they know how to recruit. That is not the case.)
- Employees that volunteered to go because the event is at their alma mater and they wanted to go back and visit
- A new employee that recently graduated from the school because some companies believe this helps create an environment that seems more approachable to candidates
- Even a past summer intern or co-op students that are still in school

So you see, you can have a wide variety of recruiting experience levels behind the booth or even interviewing you. What is usually the case is that there is one professional college recruiter leading the campus team. This is shocking, isn't it? I am essentially telling you that most people behind the booth are not professional college recruiters. Their recruiting experience may often be limited to one recruiting trip a year. Now, of course, you may find an exception to this rule here, but it will be just that, an exception. With every recruiting season, in the last ten plus years, I can count on one hand the number of times when there was more than one professional full-time college recruiter at any one college recruiting event.

For example, what if an employee with a company goes out to the same college campus for last five years as part of the campus recruiting team? When asking that person, "How many years of experience do you have college recruiting?" they might answer, "five years." But, in reality, they have only gone out to one college recruiting event, at the same college for the last five years. Now they may be a good recruiter, but my argument is how can they grow their recruiting skills with such a limited exposure even if they have the basic training? How can they consistently pick out the very best candidates when they have so little practice and so much time between that practice? It has been my experience that most cannot consistently do it.

In my experience, the smaller the company usually means the more experienced the reps are at college recruiting; but not always. That is logical if you think about it because they usually have a smaller budget, go to fewer events, and, therefore have one or two of the same people doing all their events. That means they get a lot of experience and practice. However, with larger companies? It's a totally different story. They usually go to a lot more events and need a lot more people to help at those events; often, many of those people lack the experience.

This is why I am very comfortable with saying there are as many poor recruiters out there as there are good ones, simply for the fact that many don't do it enough to have the experience and practice needed to develop into good or great recruiters. This is reality. And the reality is that recruiting is a talent and a skill that needs to be practiced often to get better. It is the experience and repetition that is critical for recruiters to develop the skills and techniques that enable them to wade through a sea of candidates to find the very best ones, consistently. It takes a substantial and continuous amount of practice and learning to grow and get better. How can you get better if you only do it once a year? Even a better question: How can you call someone a recruiter that only does it once a year?

Now you might be asking, "Why is this important to me?" It is important because it helps you understand the importance of preparing for poor or inexperience people that are functioning in some capacity as a college recruiter. If you get one of them, which again I figure is about a fifty-fifty chance, you need to ensure you do everything you can to prevent *them* from making a mistake. I know, I know, this blows away some of what you thought to be true about those that represent themselves as college recruiters on campus, so let me explain it a little more by giving you another example.

- Let's say you approach the Career Fair booth or even get selected for an interview, and the person on the other side of the table is just inexperienced. They might ask you a question and like most student answers, you give them incomplete information that lacks enough detail. This is why good and great recruiters are trained to ask follow up or what are called, "probing questions." Recruiters need to get enough detail in your answers to assess the attributes they are trying to screen for. Follow up or probing questions help them do that. But what if, like most candidates do every year, you give an answer to the recruiter that is incomplete? If that is the case, the recruiter didn't get enough information to accurately assess your answer or the attributes they are looking for and scoring you on. And, what if the recruiter doesn't know how or why they should ask a probing question? Guess what happens? Yes, you are right! They score you on the incomplete answer you gave, and it's a low score.

This is an example of exactly why I teach students and give seminars across the country. Candidates need to format their answers in a way so no matter what the experience level or training of the recruiter or interviewer, the candidates gives a complete answer that needs no probing or follow up questions. This is also why I train recruiters. They need to know that most students, year in and year out, will not give them enough detail in their answers. The recruiter needs to know how to ask probing, follow-up questions to get the detail they need to fairly assess a candidate's answer. However, I can train all I want, but I can't be in the room or at the booth to hear what everyone says. That is why the candidate needs to take the responsibility of preparing.

Now please don't be one of those students who've asked a probing question by some company representative and freak out because you realized you made a mistake by not giving them a complete answer or enough detail. No need to freak out because if they asked it, chances are they know what they are doing, you've got a good recruiter, and they probably got the detail they need.

That is just one example. There are dozens more I could give you but the point is, *you* have to make up for the lack of experience and even compensate for the poor recruiting skills the person on the other side of the table may have. To do this, you need to prepare and practice what you will learn in this book.

STORY: Are you wondering how is it possible that approximately 50% of the people behind the table at the Career Fair and even behind the interview table may not have enough training or experience to really know what they are doing? There is a pretty simple explanation. It all comes down to money. Traditionally recruiting is thought of as a Human Resource (HR) function or is based out of the HR department; this is not always the case, but is most of the time. At most companies, Human Resource departments fall under what they refer to as "Overhead," "Indirect Budget," or "Indirect Expense." This is an expense not directly linked to the product or service a company provides; if it was, it would be called a "Direct" expense. To put it another way, the expenses of all recruiting functions come right off the profit. That is a very simple explanation but an accurate one. So when companies need to cut costs, the first place they always look are those places that come out of Indirect Budget.

A trained, skilled college recruiter is expensive. It takes a lot of training, a lot of experience, a lot of time before someone becomes a great lead college recruiter. So what do companies do? Simple answer to that question: To save money and reduce indirect budget, they supplement the campus recruiting team with other people in the company. Those people may or may not have any recruiting experience. At the very best, they might go out to a couple of events per year. It is exactly like when an accountant temporarily hires administrative help around tax time. For the most part, they don't know how to do taxes, but the accountant has to have the help because of the volume of business during that time. That being said, I am not stating that these people aren't good or even great recruiters. I have many that I have trained (or that have trained me) that go out to campus with me once or twice a year, and they are nothing short of outstanding recruiters that can consistently wade through a sea of candidates and find the very top talent. However, those are few and far between. Realistically, chances are slim that those company reps that are supplementing the trip have the experience and skill to really know what they are doing.

So the point of this story is to illustrate to you who is really behind the booth and the interview table so you understand that you need to be prepared for whoever you get. Prepare for the bad or inexperienced recruiters, and the good and great ones will be easy. It is impossible for one lead recruiter to do everything on campus. They need help. They need bodies to deal with the sheer number of students they meet and events they need to attend. Where they get these bodies is wherever they can get them. At some schools and events, it is easy. Many want to go. At others, it is nearly impossible to get someone so whoever you can get, you use.

Championing candidates is a big part of our job as College Recruiters, and it is the part that takes the most time, the most work, the most motivation and dedication on our part. But what does "championing candidates" really mean? Simply put, it means that a candidate has impressed us so much, that we personally go out and sell them to managers in the company. Essentially, we take this person on as a project with the end state being getting this candidate into our company. **Your goal is to impress a recruiter enough so they will feel compelled to champion you.**

Different companies give college recruiters different levels of power. For example, several years ago I could actually hire people if they did outstanding in the interview. But times have changed for the most part. Companies are using online processes more and more. But in general, the larger the company, the more steps everyone has to go through to get a candidate in the door. That has stayed fairly consistent.

College Students: DO THIS! GET HIRED!

Everyone seems to think that college recruiters can wave a magic wand, and the job offers just start coming. But that is not the case in the vast majority of companies. Often times, they have processes they must follow. But really, what do you have to know to represent yourself as a college recruiter on campus? Some would say very little. Really, if you think about it, how much brainpower does it take to look like you know what you are doing and to ask and answer student's questions? Plus, all the students think those behind the booth know what they are doing because, well, they are behind the booth at the career fair or behind the table at the interview. I have to admit, there are members on my teams that don't know what they are doing yet. BUT, they are learning, and I am teaching. It is a skill to pick great candidates out of hundreds that you see. It takes practice. Early on in my career, I used to think I was a great recruiter because I was willing to put in the time and extra work. I have since learned that each year I gain that much more knowledge. Each year I become that much better.

By far, the most important tool that recruiters have in championing candidates and getting them into the company is their reputation. It is their reputation of consistently finding great candidates. As a lead recruiter, I am judged by the quality of the candidates I recommend as well as the quality of the candidates recommended by those I have taught. For example, managers remember if I recommended someone great, and, if I did, they will trust me again. But I could give a manager 100 great people and one average or, heaven forbid, one poor one slips through, and they will remember that one forever. So my reputation as a recruiter is on the line with each and every candidate I recommend. If I don't consistently find great candidates, hiring managers will no longer trust my judgment and, therefore, less of the candidates I recommend will get in. In a sense, we have a similar healthy fear as a hiring manager, which is we just don't want to recommend someone that is going to be a problem or has the wrong attitude. That is one of the reasons why I believe I have seen a lot of turnover in college recruiting. Each year you have to re-establish your reputation, candidate by candidate. This is very challenging, frustrating, and even infuriating at times.

Chapter 3

Resumes

Not the same old advice every other book gives you. Included are 3 Killer Tips most students don't know that will really help you stand out in a positive way.

What can I possibly tell you about writing your resume that has not been written about or sited at most every college career center and in almost every "How to Write a Resume" book? I even hesitate to put this section first because you, the reader, might think this going to just be review of what you already know or have read a thousand times before. It won't be I can assure you.

> *The way most students approach their resume writing is completely OBSOLETE! Did you know the structure of your resume is equally as important as the content?*

Resume writing as most people know it and practice it today is obsolete. Yes, there are still some good books out there that give you valuable information, and for the most part career centers do a good job at giving you the basics of putting a good looking resume together.

But, in reality, there is a paradigm shift in how to prepare a resume, and few people have seen it or are talking about it. In reality, resume writing is now married with the online application process. However, to keep things in some logical sequence, I have put it here.

I used to subscribe to the belief that when evaluating a resume, the substance or content was the most important thing, and the structure or format was a distant second. That seems very logical. After all, if a candidate had a great GPA, great leadership experience, great work experience, etc...who really cares about the location of the information on the resume as long as it was there? Well, things have shifted in the past few years with the advent and dominance of the online application processes. Now, the structure or format is **equally** as important as the content or substance. I could even put up a pretty good argument that it is more important! That's right! Stop the presses! Some crazy college recruiter just said that the substance of your resume is no more important than the structure....and it's TRUE! I will explain why.

If you are starting from scratch with your resume, my advice is simple. Go to the career center at your school and pick up an example of a good resume. Then, create one just like it with your information. That should be considered your "Base Resume." Like in constructing a house, this is your foundation of information. If you already have a resume, and have gotten it checked over already, use that as your base resume. This is the resume you can hand out to people for general purposes.

Now take that resume and see if you can implement some of the killer tips and tricks below. These tips and tricks will turn your average resume into a great one and will no doubt assist you in standing out and telling your story better. Too many times, I have met a candidate, looked over their resume and talked to them, only to discover that their resume doesn't even come close to representing how great they are.

KILLER TIP #1: Hours of Work Experience

This is a huge mistake that the vast majority of students, who work while going to school, make. How is the recruiter supposed to know how many hours you work a week? Yes, you have your "WORK EXPERIENCE" section on your resume, and it lists where you work and what your responsibilities are. But where is the number of hours you work per week? It's not there! Which means if you work 40 hours a week while going to school full time, the recruiter thinks you work a few hours a week and no more then the next person in line who has a similar experience listed. *This is an insane mistake that often represents you as just some other candidate.*

So here is the rule: If you work 20 hours a week or more, STATE IT! But state it this way: "**Worked 30 hours/week while attending school full time**" However, don't put this sentence down under WORK EXPERIENCE! Put it under

EDUCATION and close to your GPA. Why you might be asking? Simple psychology... let me explain: Let's say you are a recruiter. You have one interview slot left. You have two resumes left, both the same major from the same school. One candidate is a 3.2 GPA but worked 30 hours a week while attending school full time and put it down as I instructed above. The other is a 3.4 GPA who doesn't work at all. Who would you pick? Well, if you said the one person with a 3.2 GPA, you are right. Look at what that one sentence tells me. It tells me the person is a great time manager, they're used to being busy, they're motivated, and they're willing to work hard and make necessary sacrifices to achieve what is important to them. It tells me they have already developed a good, strong work ethic...because not many people can maintain a 3.2 GPA and work that many hours a week.

I am not here to argue whether this is the truth about this candidate. It may not be. But from my experience, chances are, it is. That is why the 3.2 GPA candidate gets the last interview slot. But without this sentence, it is really unclear who would get the interview. It has been my experience, however, that everything else being close to equal, the one with the higher GPA get's it every time. You put this sentence close to your GPA because you want to let the recruiter know that the GPA is relative. If someone has a 2.8 GPA but worked full time while holding down 18 credit hours each semester, that is worth a closer look by the recruiter. In other words, the 2.8 GPA doesn't automatically count them out. Although I disagree with this practice of counting people out for GPA alone, realistically GPA is the easiest way to decide if a candidate is in or out. It is the standby. In some cases, it is a crutch for recruiters who have not developed the skills to see greatness in people past a GPA. Don't allow them to do it to you. If you work while going to school, put down the hours per week under the education section. Even if you have a great GPA, use this trick. It could make a huge difference!

KILLER TIP #2: GPA Tricks and Tips

So while we are talking about GPA, **let's give you some tricks you can use if your GPA is a little low.** For some reason, recruiters are stuck on 3.0 being the lower limit of what they will consider. Some are very direct and up front about it, but most will just dismiss you in their heads as soon as they see anything below a 3.0. For this reason, it is important to combat that the best you can. However, please remember that these tricks will also help you if your GPA is in the lower and mid three's as well.

First, if your Cumulative GPA or (CGPA) is lower than a 3.0, try calculating your major GPA. If that is higher, put it down as Major GPA 3.4. If your CGPA and major GPA is below 3.0, take at look at your last year in school. If it is higher than 3.0, put it down like this, Junior Year GPA 3.2. If all those GPAs are below 3.0, you can calculate your last full semester GPA and hopefully that is above a 3.0 so you can put it down as, Last Semester GPA 3.2. Past that, there is really only one thing I can think of: Own it!

> *98 times out of 100 you should put your GPA on your resume. If it is low, embrace it and come up with solid story to explain why it is low to the recruiter.*

The mistake that most students make with a lower than 3.0 and even those in the low three's, is that they shy away from it or feel like they need to hide from it. Ironically, the exact opposite is what they need to do. Embrace it. Be up front with it. Above all, have the story to explain why it is low, ready to go. I understand this is hard for those out there that have lower GPAs because with a low GPA often comes a lower confidence level and in extreme cases an inferiority complex. **What I am telling you is to stop playing defense and switch to offense. Embrace the low GPA. Don't hide it. Don't be scared of it. Talk about it and put it out there right away with recruiters.** But make sure you have developed a smooth, organized, and compelling story to explain why it is low. As discussed in the Interview Chapter, you must have Situation, Behavior, and Outcome in that story, and you must take the initiative and tell the story right at the beginning of your conversation. For example: At the Career Fair, if you have a low GPA, acknowledge it right away and then break right into your story. You will be amazed at how good this works and will be equally amazed at how much better you feel about it. After teaching this to students, I have seen them try it and get huge success. Plus in some, it fundamentally changes the way they feel about it, which in turn gives them more confidence. This translates into a better impression on the recruiter. Just try it. You have nothing to lose and everything to gain.

Put your GPA on your resume. Just do it! There are many more disadvantages of not having it on, than advantages of not having it on. Moreover, some career centers are telling their students to leave off their GPA on their resume if it is below a certain level. This is a HUGE mistake and not the right information to give to students. I strongly disagree with this advice and believe that, in the vast majority of cases, it is just wrong! However, if it is really low even after all these tricks above, let's say 2.5 or below, that is when I might leave it off.

STORY: Recently, I was recruiting at University of Central Florida. I was working the Career Fair booth, and a young woman who was a finance major approached me. It was lunch time so I had a little more time to spend with her since the line was not long. I read over her resume. She had a 3.2 GPA, was a senior, and was looking for a full time position. She had no internship or co-op experience. Her resume was average at best but nothing really exciting. I asked her if she had applied online yet and she said no, so I went into my script about how she needs to apply online while looking over her resume a little more. Then I noticed she worked at a hotel and I had no one waiting, so I started to ask her about that. You would not believe what I discovered. She worked 45 or more hours a week, every week at this hotel, managing all the housekeeping staff. She did this while attending school full time with more than a full time load of credit hours each semester. She told me how she was paying for her entire education herself with no help from anyone. Sometimes, she would be called in late at night to resolve a dispute or to fill in for someone who didn't show, and then she would go right to class with no sleep. This woman was nothing less than impressive. I granted her an interview the next day, (she had to take an hour off of work to do it and asked me if it would be ok if she could come in her work clothes but offered to dress in a suit. I, of course, told her no problem on wearing the work clothes) and let me tell you....the best interview of the day in any major! She had so many good examples and stories to answer the questions. Then, after the interview, I spent another 15 minutes with her helping her fix her resume. What a difference those fifteen minutes made.

The point is her resume didn't represent her well at all. It didn't give me her story accurately. It didn't convey the great experience she had nor did it represent all the sacrifices she made to get her education. She was nothing more than an average candidate on her resume, but in reality, she was extraordinary. Her new resume got her a ton of attention when she was getting little to none before.

KILLER TIP #3: Leadership

One thing I see year after year is a section on a candidate's resume entitled ACTIVITES, or HOBBYS/CLUBS or something similar. Do you really think recruiters care about this? Now before I get a bunch of nasty e-mails saying things like, "There is great value in knowing someone's activities because it is a great indicator of how well rounded a candidate is," let me explain. You have a few objectives when writing your resume. One would be to impress   with your resume. Everyone would agree with that. Another one might be to inspire a recruiter's curiosity so they engage you. That would be true as well. However, the primary objective is for you to tell the story about yourself. In this story, you want to give them some strong indicators that you have the ***attributes*** they are looking for; that you are the kind of person they what to hire. Every section in your resume should reflect this. The section called "Activities" is ok, but does it really support the primary objective? It might in the content under activities, but the word "Activities" is weak. It is more of a passive word.

So what should you do? Take a look at what you have under "Activities." Most of the time, when I teach a resume writing class, I look at a student's resume under activities, and I see some great leadership experience. So instead of the heading "Activities," why don't you put LEADERSHIP? Do you see how much more powerful the word "leadership" is compared to the word "activities"? Plus.... and here is the most powerful reason..., **"Leadership" is an *attribute* they are looking for and "Activities" is not.**

Here is another thing about the leadership section when I do see it. I notice two mistakes that students consistently make. One, they put their leadership experience in chronological order. All I can say to this is that it is not the most effective way. The most effective way is for you to put your highest position first. For example, if you are now Treasurer of a major student club and last year you were the President of a smaller club, put the President position first. Why? Because with one word, you convey that you were not only a leader, but you were the top leader. So put your titles in order of strength. The word President first followed by Vice President second, and so on.

The second mistake I often see is the way candidates present the information. For example, they were President of a club, but in the bullet item they insist in putting the name of the club first along with a short description and maybe even the time period they served ...then at that end, the title they held which was President. This is the wrong way to do it! The most powerful word in that bullet is the word "President," so put it first. **Give the recruiter what they want to see first.**

Lastly, and this is just purely psychological...having the word "Leadership" as a heading automatically puts the recruiter in the mindset that you are a leader. I know that seems a little farfetched or over simplified, but it is not. By giving them that heading of "Leadership," you are giving them a strong indicator that you have an attribute that they are looking for; which directly supports the primary objective.

For those of you who are fortunate enough to have some kind of security clearance, have a separate heading that says "CLEARANCE." Then, list your security clearance. However, because I have recruited for both secret and top secret programs, before you show your resume to anyone, run it by the security department in the organization that got you that clearance. This is very important to make sure the way you list your clearance on your resume is appropriate.

Make sure when you apply online to create a section at the bottom of your resume called "Interest Areas." What you put in this section are the key words and phrases that are in the job(s) you are applying to. To learn more about how to do this, I give a detailed explanation in the Applying Online chapter.

STORY: Very early on in my recruiting career, there was a young woman engineer from Embry-Riddle Aeronautical University who got an internship but only had a 2.7 GPA. At that time, I was not at all involved with the selection process since I was so new. I was very surprised that she was selected since all those around her had significantly higher GPA's which was typical of the candidates that got hosen for internships. (I am not saying those with a 2.7 or a low GPA have nothing to offer, but it is just harder, a lot harder I have learned, for them to compete because there are so many 3.7s available. Plus, let's face it, all things being equal, if you are an engineering manager looking to fill a position and you have a ton of candidates to pick from, the easiest way to count someone out is to take out those with the lowest GPAs. This happens all the time. Whether anyone agrees or disagrees with this is not the issue. It happens and will continue to happen. More times than not, it is the hiring manager that makes the final decision as to what candidate to hire. It is a daunting task when you have dozens if not hundreds of candidates to choose from. The easiest way to reduce that down is to simply count out those below a certain GPA.) When her internship was done, she really wanted a full time offer. However, some people around me really didn't think we should push for her getting a full-time offer. I did. The reason I did was because I investigated her performance from those she worked for and worked with. All of them agreed that she was not the most technical, but no one ever out-worked her. She would come in early, stay late. If she didn't know how to solve a problem or get an answer, she would find a way to get the information she needed to resolve the issue. Plus, she always followed up, always keeping people in the loop. But above all, everyone liked her because of her positive "can do" attitude. She never complained. Whatever assignment she got she approached it with a positive attitude. She was always willing to volunteer to take on the assignments no one else wanted. She brought an infectious, uplifting attitude to every group, every team, and every person she worked with. She won over even the most skeptical people. These were some really technical people. They knew she wasn't the most technical person. They knew there were many others stronger than she was from a technical perspective. But they all wanted to work with her, and they always wanted her on their team.

With me pushing her and with that reputation, she got hired full time by one of the hardest bosses I had experienced at that time. He was a genius and very technical. He didn't like anyone he didn't know well which included me; later we became friends. He was extremely demanding and hardly ever satisfied with anyone's work. I remember talking to him a year after she worked for him. He stated, "She is the best employee I have." Remember, attitude is everything.

Chapter 4

Career Fair

Getting an interview is why you attend the career fair so how to do it is spelled out for you. Includes 3 Huge Tips that could, on their own, get you the interview.

So why is the Career Fair so important? After all, most of the time students feel as if they stand in line (sometimes 30 minutes, especially with the larger companies) just to talk to a company representative who then basically tells them to go apply on the website. What a waste of time right? Wrong! Look, when you boil it down, the Career Fair is a chance to be seen; a chance to impress. Yes, the odds are not in your favor when there are dozens of students in line trying to do the same thing. But let's approach it another way. Let's break it down to what I like to call, "The Prime Directive," or your number one priority for being there.

My job here is to transfer your stress. Most candidates, especially in this job market, go to a Career Fair with the stress of performing well enough just to bet one interview with one company. I can't take away that stress, but hopefully, instead, I can transfer it to you being stressed over the fact that you have so many interviews with multiple companies.

First, there are some HUGE tricks and tips I will tell you that will make you stand out at any company, no matter how many people are in line. These tricks have proven to be very effective by students I have taught, across the US at colleges and universities from coast to coast. But they are rarely used and I always wondered why for years; until I discovered that students just don't know about them. I am surprised that many students are not quite sure what their number one priority is at the Career Fair. Yes, they want to impress company reps in hopes to get hired.... but hold on! That sounds right, but you're missing a big step. Simply put, your number one priority should be ...TO GET AN INTERVIEW! It is not to get a job! At least not yet. What company would talk to you for 3 minutes at the Career Fair booth and then just offer you a job without an interview?

Of course, there are a couple of exceptions. For example, freshmen or sophomores who are not familiar with what companies want or what is out there may come to the Career Fair to learn what it is all about; to get the lay of the land. That's fine. It is actually more than fine. It is an excellent idea that I encourage all underclassman to do. But I would argue that they are still linked into The Prime Directive. They are learning how to work the event. They are learning what they are in for so when they are ready, they have the tools to put their best foot forward and score an interview. Another exception is people that go just to get the FREE giveaways. But they clearly are not in the demographic recruiters are looking for. OK, so let me take you through the Career Fair step by step. You should have plenty of copies of your resume. You should be dressed up in your interview clothes...please understand: to recruiters, the Career Fair is mini interview or a short screening interview. Your job is to impress them enough so that they send you to the next step. For many companies, that is an interview for the next day on campus. But that is not always the case. For some, it may be a phone interview at some time in the future. **But the bottom line: your job is to impress the recruiter enough so that they will want to send you to the next step in the process, the interview.**

But how do you do that with so many people trying to do the same thing? Well, there are some specific things you can do to greatly enhance your chances. For example, having a past performance evaluation to give to the recruiters behind the booth is CRAZY effective; it needs to be good of course. In the upcoming chapter on

Interviewing, one of the key mantras widely accepted in the interview literature is that past performance is a good indicator of future performance. I would agree. That is why they usually ask you questions that are "behavioral" in the interview. **Recruiters want to hear about what you have done in the past because it is a gauge of how you will perform in the future.** But what does that have to do with the Career Fair? Well, remember, I said the time in front of the company rep at the booth is a mini interview.

HUGE TIP #1: Bring Past Performance Evaluations and your "A" Game

So now, you show up to the Career Fair booth. You are dressed properly, and you are prepared. However, so are most of those great candidates in line with you...and not everyone is going to succeed at The Prime Directive (to get an interview) because there is a limited number of interview slots. For example, at the Career Fair booth, I pick probably one out of every ten to fifteen candidates to interview. But you don't have to worry about that. You have something extra. You have something that will most assuredly show them they should take a chance on you and give you an interview. You have something that will reduce their fear of making the mistake of picking the wrong person. **This something is a copy of your past performance evaluation. This is HUGE!** What is more powerful than handing them your resume and then handing them a past performance evaluation that is excellent? There are very few tips or tricks that have this level of effectiveness at changing a recruiter's mind set over to your side so quickly.

I cannot express to you how powerful this is. Again, as we talked about, recruiting is not an exact science. It is not a hard science like a mathematical equation where it is either a right or wrong answer. Yes, we have official interview forms that quantifiably score each person on the same set of criteria. But there is no way, I repeat, *no way* to take all the subjectivity out of the equation. In this situation, you are at the Career Fair. Your job is to impress the recruiter enough to get an interview. By you offering a written document from another

41

company or by your past boss, illustrating that you are a top performer and that your past work has been great, means not only are you well prepared, but you have shown the recruiter you are willing to take the extra step; go the extra mile. You are proud of your past work and your past performance, and you are essentially saying to the recruiter, "This is the kind of performance you can expect if you help me get into your company." **JACKPOT!** By providing them a copy of a past performance evaluation, you have shown them you are not just another candidate. You have shown them that the risk they have in choosing you for an interview and potential job is low. You have shown them that you are prepared and have the right attitude. Try it! You have nothing to lose and everything to gain. **This just might be that one thing that gets you the interview!**

The best performance evaluations are those that are quantifiable; in other words, they score you on a scale of numbers. Also, they need to be signed by your manager or your boss. A letter of recommendation is NOT a performance evaluation and it is not quantifiable. It is not the same thing nor does it carry even close to the same weight. As a matter of fact, it carries very little weight simply because I know it is going to put you in a positive light. But a performance evaluation scores or ranks you in many performance areas. It just doesn't simply say you were great, it tells the story of your greatness across many categories.

HUGE TIP #2: Listen for the questions

You are prepared, you have plenty of copies of your resume and your past performance evaluation, and you are standing in line waiting to talk to the recruiter. Why is it that while standing in line most candidates talk to their friends, talk on their cell phone, text message, and look around seemingly in a daze, etc...? Then, when you get up to the booth, you do your best at answering the questions we ask you. But what if there was a way for you to know the questions we are going to ask you *before* you get up to the booth. Well there is! Here's how:

While standing in the line of companies that are at the top of your list to work for, listen to the questions that the recruiters are asking the candidates ahead of you. This is simple yet brilliant! Why? Because recruiters for the most part develop a script or set of questions they like to ask all candidates at the Career Fair. This is human nature. Do you think we make up new questions for everyone we see? Well, we don't. In general, we stick to the same few questions for each candidate. That is why if you listen to the questions we are asking the candidates ahead of you, we will probably ask you the same ones or some of the same ones. In the Career Fair seminar that I teach when I go out on campuses, I even go as far as telling the students that before they stand in line, to approach the booth casually and to listen to the questions. Then write them down. Next, go to the end of the line and while you are waiting, formulate your answers. If you are not comfortable with that, after you listen to the questions, walk to some quiet corner of the room and formulate your answers. Then, get back in line and practice them until you are next. If you don't like either of those methods, get a friend to do some reconnaissance for you. Have them causally listen in on the questions and report back to you. Now that I think about it, you could even hire a freshman for like $3 to go up to the booth and ask the recruiter what questions they normally ask candidates. Freshmen come to the booth all the time asking what we look for in candidates and what they should do to prepare for a future job with us, questions like this.

Yes, there are times when we see something on your resume that we ask specifically about, but it is usually something positive that we picked up on. Also, at booths that have little traffic, the recruiters have a lot more time to spend so they might ask you more questions...but that is because they have time because they don't have a lot of people coming to their booth. So now you have even less competition, and those tips I have mentioned still are extremely effective.

HUGE TIP #3: Ask for an Interview

This tip is probably the most effective tip I have seen used successfully many, many times but only if you do it the right way. Don't make the mistake of thinking that if you just ask for an interview, you will get one, although you might. **You have to both do it at the right time and use the right words.** This is the key! Here is how: You did both Huge Tip #1 & #2 and you are talking to the recruiter. Chances are that if you followed both tips before this one, the recruiter is just signing you up for an interview. But what if that has not happened yet and the conversation is winding down? Let's say the recruiter starts to say something like, "Well, you have some really good things on your resume. Make sure you go apply online, and you have a good chance at getting noticed." Then, the recruiter reaches out his/her hand to shake yours. What this means is that you didn't get an interview, and they are trying to politely conclude with you and get on to the next person.

But wait! You still have a great opportunity to get an interview. This is when you use the best tip. I would call it a "Hail Mary" play, but it is much more effective than that. This is exactly what you say, **"I would really appreciate an interview with you tomorrow. If you grant me an interview, I promise I won't let you down."** POWERFUL! Read it again but read it slow. Do you see the emotion? Do you see that it is not only a personal plea but a promise you are making to that recruiter? This is psychology, and it works!

You have now infused emotion into the equation. You have gotten the recruiter out of their script and out of their comfort zone and you, in two sentences, made it personal. You made yourself the underdog. Everyone loves to root for the underdog. I have seen how effective it is because I came up with it and I have taught it. You would not believe how successful this technique is. What do you have to lose? Nothing! You were being told to go to the website. You were done. But then you came *thundering back* with this statement. You changed the game. It works! **Just do it!**

STORY: Recently, I was recruiting at University of Florida, and I was scheduled to teach two seminars: one on the secrets of applying online and the other on how to negotiate salary. Well, so many people showed up to each of them that they had to turn people away. Because there was an hour between the different seminars, the organization in charge asked me if I would give back-to-back seminars. I ended up teaching several hundred students that day at four seminars. In the last seminar, in the question and answer portion, one guy asked me to give him my best tip for getting an interview from the Career Fair the next day. I told him and the rest of the audience, the Huge Tip #3 above. The next day, near the end of the career fair, that same guy came up to me at the booth. He introduced himself, and I told him I remembered him from the day before. He told me he just stopped by to thank me. He said that last semester he went to the career fair and did not get one interview. He then said he used my advice I just gave him the day before. He said he now had several interviews the next day and was very excited. He admitted that he felt a little stressed because he had so many and was anxious to get home to prepare. Finally, he said he felt he should stop by and let me know the success he had by following my advice, even though my company didn't have the job he wanted. Then he thanked me again and left. This kind of situation happens every time I teach a seminar before the career fair. He was the fourth person that day to come up to the booth and thank me for the advice. Each had great success, and so will you if you just try it.

Look, the chance of you *not* scoring an interview if you follow these **three HUGE TIPS** is slim. I am not giving you 20 tips to follow. I am simply giving you the top three that I know work most of the time. Even if you just use one of these tips, your chances of getting an interview greatly increase because you made yourself stand out in a positive way. You did something that most candidates at the Career Fair just do not do. In a sea of students, you stand out in a positive way. Those are the people that get interviews.

Now you might ask me:

- Do I approach small, medium, and large companies the same?
- Don't I change my approach significantly when I am talking

  with a small company as opposed to the large company?
- Having the same approach for different sized
  companies can't possibly work, can it?

I hear questions like this all the time. In my career as a college recruiter, I have been involved in the recruiting process for small, medium and large companies. Why is it that candidates feel like there is something they need to change in their approach just because of the size of a company? For the most part, the approach is exactly the same. Your job is to put your best foot forward. Stand out in a positive way. Be prepared and follow up. Why would a recruiter from a small, medium, or large company be looking for anything different? Now maybe they are looking for different skills, but if you think about it, all recruiters want the best candidates they can find. So why change your approach?

> *Whether you are trying to acquire a job at a small, medium, or large company your approach basically stays the same.*

Yes there are small differences. For example, at Career Fairs, some of the big companies have three booth spaces and a dozen recruiters. They have huge lines that sometimes you are waiting in for thirty minutes or more. On the other hand, I have seen small and even medium-sized companies have no lines and just one booth with just one or two company representatives. If you are approaching those booths, obviously, you can't listen for the question they are asking someone in front of you in line, when there is no line. Moreover, since there is a short or no line at all, the recruiters will have the luxury of spending more time with you; asking you more questions and talking with you more. However, this gives you a great chance to stand out

46

because you have even less competition. **But recruiters look for the same things. They look for the best candidates no matter what size the company is.**

That being said, in general, the smaller the company the more time they have to evaluate each candidate, and the more time they take reading each candidate's resume. I remember when I was involved with recruiting for a small company; I would read everything only because there were not a lot of applicants. I read every line of the resume and even read the cover letter. But when recruiting for a big company, I have many, many more people to consider. I had to change my process to more of a scanning of the resume only, at least initially. Either way, you win because you are prepared more than every other candidate. If it is a big company, they have more candidates to look at and less time to spend with each one. They will most likely give interviews to the ones that quickly impress them. In smaller companies, they will normally have fewer candidates to pick from and will spend a little more time with each candidate. They will pick those candidates that impress them the most. Whichever is the case, you will be one of those candidates if you follow the upcoming advice.

Chapter 5

Interviews

I teach you one easy to remember method that really works. I walk you through it step by step. Also, I give you 3 Crazy Good tips and tell you the most effective way to follow up.

How do you know that you did badly in an interview? What if you are making the same mistake in every interview with every company, and that mistake is preventing you from getting an offer? The only way you will know this is if you go to your career center and do mock interviews. That way, the professional counselors will be able to spot it and help you correct it. But it still doesn't answer the question, "So what does it really take to be a great interviewee; to really impress an interviewer?" Again, over 10 years of interviewing thousands of college students leads me to what you will learn in this section. There are many elements. We can discuss body language, how to dress, what to do if you have sweaty palms, basically, all those topics you find in many of the other "How To" interview books that are a billion pages long. Many of those topics are helpful. But can I just assume that you know these things or will find out how to address them before you interview so we can get down to business? For example, the subject of dressing appropriately. After

> *There is a crazy amount of information out there on interviewing. I boil it down and tell you what you need to know and what works best!*

all, your choice of tie or color of pantsuit is really low on the totem pole when it comes to scoring huge in an interview. Yes, yes....you need to dress correctly, conservatively. That means guys, have a suit and tie (a boring tie...you know...the kind your grandfather would wear or the kind you would wear to a funeral... not a Mickey Mouse or Hooters' tie). Girls, wear a nice boring pantsuit. What I usually say to the girls in my seminars, when I briefly mention this, is to go into your closet and get the most boring outfit you have and wear that. But that is not going to get you the job; however, it might blow it for you if you dress like an idiot...so stick with advice your Career Center gives you on this topic. You need to show the interviewer that you can "Play Ball" which means you understand that in the interview environment you need to fit in when it comes to dress....not stand out. For some of you, that might mean taking a few of your facial piercings out and limiting them to an even baker's dozen or so (did you catch my sarcasm?). Those of you that might have a bunch of facial piercings please don't email me outlining why this is biased conspiracy against you that goes against your rights of freedom of expression. I understand. I get it. But I am telling you what you should do to put your best foot forward, period. I am not trying to be politically correct in hopes that you will read between the lines and somehow pick up on what I am trying to tell you. I am just telling you what works. For example, you and I don't know what biases the interviewer may have...in this case, piercing. Remember, your goal is to do everything you can to show them you are great, you will fit in, and you won't be a problem. Also, remember that your boss, on many occasions, may be old enough to be your parent. That often means they have different views of the world and what may or may not be appropriate or acceptable. (Wow, that last sentence really sounded politically correct; which is rare for me. So for those of you that do better with a little more direct approach, here is another way to put it: Don't be an idiot. Be polite, be professional, dress appropriately, and fit in.)

Again, the number one fear of hiring managers and recruiters is hiring someone who is a problem. So, if you start off the interview dressed inappropriately, do you see how that can translate into the interviewer being less inclined to recommend you? It throws up a red flag right away and puts you in a potential uphill battle. Plus, it is a first impression. You need to ensure it is a good one or you may not ever recover.

STORY: One late October, early in my career, I was at Rensselaer Polytechnic Institute (RPI) in Troy NY, and I was doing fall recruiting for my company. Now, for those of you familiar with Troy NY in late October, well, it can be beautiful. But it can also be cold and snowy. There were about two inches of snow on the ground. At around noon, I went to lunch in the cafeteria. Many students were there. After I sat down, my mentor, Dr. Neil Campbell, (a Ph. D. in Chemical Engineering, and RPI alum) who was teaching me the ropes came in. He was with some joker who had a wrinkled suit, pretty long hair that didn't look like it had been combed, and his tie was loosened up so the tie knot was about three inches down from where it should be. They both came over and sat down with me. My immediate evaluation of the situation was that it was some student trying to impress him and following him around talking about anything and everything he can think of. As a recruiter, sometimes that happens. I then noticed that this guy wasn't even wearing socks. Two inches of snow, he took the time to wear a suit but had no socks. Not a good first impression. Dr. Campbell introduced me to him as Dave Johnson, and I shook his hand and said hello, but then I stayed out of the conversation since I was eating. Then Dave got up and left.

Not 5 minutes went by and Dr. Campbell asked me what I thought. I told him I was not that impressed and why. Then believe it or not, he asked me to put him on my interview schedule. I looked up at him with what I am sure was confusion on my face, and said, "Why?" He then answered, "Let's see what he can do."

The next day Dave showed up to his interview. Same suit; same wrinkles...and still no socks. I thought to myself, "what a waste of my time," and was less than enthusiastic about interviewing him. I mean come on, no socks with a suit? Looking back on it, I was

51

inexperienced and, basically, I had my mind made up that this guy was not the caliber of candidate my company was looking for. But I started the interview. I asked him the same questions as all the other candidates. I remember being surprised when he really answered the first question well; I mean really well. Then, the second and third questions were answered equally as well. It took me over half the interview to even start warming up to how good his answers were...all because of no socks.

Now this might seem odd or even unfair to you; me, essentially pre-judging someone because of what they wear or in this case don't wear to the interview. But do you think that is professional, him not having any socks on for the interview? Remember, one of my jobs as a recruiter is to evaluate him on whether or not he would be the right fit for my company. But Dave was exceptional. He was brilliant and yet very personable. His answers to my questions were outstanding! He knew how to answer questions in the correct format and time (which I will teach you if you keep reading). So, I had to make a choice, recommend him no socks and all or not recommend him. And this is the point. Why would I even consider not recommending him if he was that good? The point of the story is to illustrate the importance of dressing correctly. Yes, Dave overcame it because he really was exceptional. But most are not, so why put yourself into an uphill battle? Plus, do not make the assumption that those interviewing you will overlook things like no socks. Most won't!

I did highly recommend Dave, and he did get an internship with my company. If I remember correctly, I actually hired him in because at that time I was hand selecting all the interns. I also remember taking great pleasure making fun of him whenever I could work the "no socks" story in with the other interns. After he finished his undergrad, he had offers with my company but accepted a position with another company that had a position that was just a better fit. This was a huge loss for my company, but this is part of being a recruiter; you never get all those in you want or think should get in.

Some of you might know Dave. He was on one season of Survivor and was the Rocket Scientist; and he really is a Rocket Scientist. I just reconnected with him again when I saw him at a recent Career Fair at Massachusetts Institute of Technology (MIT). He left his position at the company he was working for and had gone back to school for a Master's degree and was interested in investigating full time opportunities with my company. I will definitely do whatever I can to help him get in. It is rare to find a candidate that is as good as Dave is in so many areas. And yes, he was wearing socks this time!

So, how do you prepare yourself for interviews? Can't there just be one simple way that will let you learn how to answer most if not all interview questions really well without having to memorize a bunch of stories that some book told you on how to answer questions like, "What is your greatest weakness?"

There is a way. It works. I know it works because over the past 10 years, many, many students have e-mailed me thanking me for teaching them this method. But I have boiled it down to just a few key factors. What you are really looking for is a method to help you become a great interviewee. I have taken some of what is already out there and refined it to create one focused approach for college students.

[GETTING TO THE POINT]

Most first interviews are now Behavior Interviews or sometimes called "Structural Interviews." This is commonplace now. You want to know why? Because those making the hiring decisions generally believe that past behavior and performance are great indicators of future behavior and performance; a lot of the literature supports this view. So the belief is, when you are interviewing with a company, your behavior on past assignments and at past jobs is the strongest indicator of what you will do for them. So, you must have specific examples, and they must be in the form of a story. They must be direct, succinct, organized, and structured.

53

Like I talked about in Chapter 2, "The Truth about College Recruiters", recruiters try to keep emotion out of the process of recruiting, and you really are trying to keep it in. You want to answer the questions so well, so smoothly, that the college recruiter will want to take it personal whether or not you get into the company. You want the college recruiter to champion you. If your interview answers are so good, they will take championing you personally! This is your goal.

Interviewing is nothing more than telling stories. You are essentially scored on how well you tell stories about you and your experiences. So, why is it so hard and stressful for some? Some say because it is like a test. You really never know what they are going to ask. Plus, you are talking to a complete stranger and in a small time, trying to stand out, impress, and convince them that you are "all that and a bag of chips." This is nerve-racking for some. I know it was for me when I was in your spot, but there is a solution.

There are many methods out there: STAR (Situation, Task, Action, Result), SBO (Situation, Behavior, and Outcome), SAO (Situation, Action, and Outcome), SAR (Situation, Action, and Result), and others. I don't really care which one you use, but use one of them because they are all leading you down the same correct path. I prefer SBO because the "B" stands for Behavior and that is really what is being tested in a behavioral interview. The "B" is a good reminder for you to focus on your behavior and that each question is trying to evaluate you on your past behavior.

The key to all of these methods is to prepare and to have examples in the form of a story. Any question they ask should be answered detailing: **S, B, O and should be completed in about 90 seconds.** That leaves you approximately 30 seconds for Situation, 30 seconds for Behavior, and 30 seconds for Outcome. I would say allow yourself 10 seconds total either way but no more and no less. In other words, your entire answer should lie between 80 – 100 seconds with the sweet spot at 90 seconds. If it is much shorter than this, usually there is not enough detail to warrant a really high score. If it is much longer than this, there is usually too much detail or it is not organized enough for the interviewer to quickly see what they need to. Although each section is very important and a must have to score high, **if I had to choose which one was most important, I would have to pick Behavior.** This is because all recruiters or interviewers should know what I have told you already and that is past behavior is often a good indicator of future behavior.

Here is how you get started: You should have 6 or more stories ready to go. Focus your stories on areas or topics that companies most likely will ask. Here are some:

- Leadership ✔
- Dealing with a difficult person
- Adaptability
- Helping others (without being told to do so)
- What did you do when something went wrong?
- Solving a Problem ✔
- Your Greatest Strength ✔
- Your Greatest Weakness ✔
- Your Greatest Accomplishment ✔
- Your Greatest Disappointment ✔

Now I know what you are saying: "I thought we weren't supposed to memorize answers and regurgitate them back." This is different. These are stories about your life -- your experiences. You already know them because you lived them. So really all you have to do is to tell your stories back to the interviewer in the S, B, O format. That's it! You don't have to memorize them because they are your experiences; you already know them.

What I suggest is to take a piece of paper and write down each of the topic areas above. Then put S, B, O below them and start filling in your story. Concentrate on the Situation first. Then move to Behavior, YOUR behavior. Finally, work on the Outcome. Once you have that down, all you really need to do is make sure the timing and details are in each section and you got it! Yes, you will have to practice them so they flow. Yes, it will take you an hour or two to develop and practice your stories, but that is all. Plus, you spent at least that much time on your resume, so if you just spend the same amount of time rehearsing your stories, you will do great. This is a critical step if you want success. Remember, companies hire the person, not the resume.

So you want more help developing the SBO, well I am here for you. Below are the important aspects of S, B, and O.

SITUATION (S): The Situation section is where you illustrate to the interviewer in words the environment that you are in and perhaps how you got there. You explain the scene. Your job is to paint a picture of where you are, what you are doing, what you are responsible for, the problem you need to solve, etc... **Use details.** Describe your surroundings. Describe the assignment you were given. Describe things like how many people were on your team or what class the assignment is for. Do all this in 30 seconds. If you are doing it in less than 30 seconds, most likely you need to add more details. If it is more than 30 seconds, you need to cut out some of the details and become more succinct and more organized about telling the situation.

BEHAVIOR (B): This is where you describe YOUR behavior. Not what the team did but what *you* did specifically. **This is the key section because this is what they are looking for most.** If it is the first question, the interviewer is looking for a good example of you using good judgment, good initiative, good problem solving skills, etc. Then, if you do well on that first question, on the rest of the questions they will be looking for a trend or consistency in your behavior. A tip here: If you, or your friends that you practice your stories with, think your behavior is what most people would do in a similar situation, that is a good indicator that your story is probably good at best. You want GREAT! If your behavior, as you explain it, is above and beyond what most people will do in a similar situation, now you have an excellent chance at scoring GREAT! Great candidates often go the extra mile and do one more thing than most people would do in a similar situation. **Remember, details again are the key.** You want to show the interviewer that your behaviors lead to success.

OUTCOME (O): First piece of advice here: you might want to make the outcome *positive!* I have seen 100 times how someone does well in painting a great picture in the Situation. Then, in the Behavior section goes above and beyond what the normal person would do. Then, in the Outcome section describes that the project or task they were responsible for failed, but they say they learned a lot. Talk about torpedoing the ship! Come on! If the outcome of a story is not positive, then get another story.

Now, the next step is to assist you with questions I always seem to get like, "But how do I answer questions like, "What is your greatest strength?" and "What is your greatest weakness?" These are what I like to refer to as "critical questions." That means, that it is critical for you to do well on these questions, even if it is only well enough to get through the question and on to the next one without any trouble. See, recruiters like to peer into your soul if they can. Critical questions seem to help us do that quickly because they make you almost instantly prioritize significant things about yourself and about your life. They make you pick one thing, one event, one example from all your life experiences to answer one question. That is powerful because it gives the interviewer a window into who you are. What you believe. What is important to you. What you are about. Yes, I know, it is only one question. But over an entire interview, those critical questions, and others, often act as a road map to who you are and what you will be like as an employee. Sometimes, it may give an interviewer just a glimpse of an area that they want to probe further or get clarification on. Remember, this is not an exact science. Yes, good and great interviewers try hard to just score you based on a set of criteria and nothing else. But there are always times when something just doesn't sound right or the answer to the question, the words that the candidate uses, seems to indicate that there is more there. Trained interviewers will probe those areas to make sure they have the whole picture, the whole story.

In the end, critical questions are no different than any other question when it comes down to what you need to do to answer them. Just follow the same S, B, O approach above, and you will do great.

CRAZY GOOD TIP #1: It is about what YOU did, *not* what the team did.

Don't make the mistake of answering interview questions with what the team did. I want to know what YOU did. I am not interviewing the team. I know, I know, you want me to see that you're a "team player" and can work as a part of a team. I get it. Corporate America has stressed the importance of working as a part of a team; being a team player. But I am not interviewing the team. I am interviewing you. You will have, or should have, a few stories where you functioned inside a team. Plus I don't think that anyone would admit that they are not a team player if I asked them because they know companies want good team players. The fact of the matter is, there are some candidates out there that are not good team players. Our job is to try to figure this out through your behavior illustrated to us in your answers to our interview questions.

CRAZY GOOD TIP #2: Ask For The Job!

No one ever just asks for the job and that is a tragedy because it often works. **This may be the difference between you getting the job and someone else getting it.** Asking for the job gives you an edge and makes it crystal clear that you are interested and committed. You do it at the very end, just as you are about to leave. This is what you say: *"There is one last thing I would like to ask you. I would like to ask you for the job. It sounds exciting and is just what I am looking for. I promise I will work hard for you."* Come on! Is there any question the interviewer(s) will remember you now? Look, suppose you are a little shy or a little nervous in the interview; or a lot nervous. Some of your enthusiasm about the position might be stifled because of this. You never want to leave the interviewer wondering if you really want the job. That is a sure-fire way for them to choose someone else. With the four short sentences above there will be no question in the interviewer's mind that you want the position. You will stand out! They will remember you! You have a better chance at getting the job if you just ask for it. Do this at the very end of every interview.

CRAZY GOOD TIP #3: Bring a "Cheat Sheet" to the interview

Did you know that if you are playing blackjack in Las Vegas, you can actually have with you, in plain sight, a card that tells you how to play each hand? This is totally legal, and often the casinos themselves sell these cards in their gift shops. So why don't you do the same thing in your interviews? Why don't you just bring some notes with you that remind you what your stories are? This is totally acceptable, yet few people do it. Many students worry they won't remember all their stories under pressure. This is understandable. I know many people just get really nervous and have this fear that they might "lock up". Chances are, if you prepared, you will do great and won't even need your notes, but having them there as a reminder may help. Also, in your notes, why not write S, B, O to remind yourself that on every answer, these three things need to be in your answer.

"But what if they ask me a question that doesn't fit with any of the stories I came up with?" I get asked this question from time to time. The answer is that you will find most of your stories flexible enough to answer many different questions. That is the beauty of this approach. You will discover that the answer for your greatest strength might also be a great answer for your greatest accomplishment or even dealing with a difficult person. However, if you find yourself in that situation and none of your stories seem to fit, the great thing about it is that you know what you need to do. You have practiced and are even programmed now to answer any interview question with Situation, Behavior, and Outcome. So I would recommend that in the interview you have a piece of paper and if a question comes up like that, you simply write down S,B,O to remind yourself and think about an experience you had that would answer the question. Simply start off with the situation, then move on to behavior, and, finally, the outcome. Believe me, at the very least, you will do a lot better than most.

Another questions student always ask me is, "But what if they give me one of those overly general questions?" Ok, suppose you are asked, "Tell me a little about yourself." Why does everyone panic on this question? This is GREAT! You are hoping for this question. You know why? Because it is your chance to break out your best story and tell it. All you really need to do is have a good transition or lead in like, "I think the best way to get to know me is to know what my greatest strength is. Let me give you and example." Then you just break into that story.

[WHAT YOU SHOULD ASK IN THE INTERVIEW]

There is another thing you should have in the notes you prepare and bring with you to the interview -- **questions**. Write down the questions that you should ask the interviewer. Notice how I didn't say the questions you *want* to ask. There is a difference.

I think you should ask only three questions and then ask for the job. You are at the end of the interview process, and the interviewer is asking you if you have any questions. This is the perfect opportunity to finish strong so you should phrase your first question in a way that tries to impress the interviewer one last time. **(How you do that is starting with a statement of specific fact about the company followed by a question relating to that fact.)** For example, "I noticed you recently acquired XYZ Company into your research and development group. How will that increase your market share globally?" The strategy here is so start off with a statement that shows you did your homework about the company. The statement part of the question shows you took the initiative to research the company, that you went the extra mile. Asking the question was not really about getting the answer to the question. It was about giving them one more example, right at the end of the interview, of what they can expect if they hire you. They may not even know the answer, and you don't really care. Your job was to show them, one last time, that you were both prepared and researched the company. **This should be your first question.**

The second question should verify the interviewer's contact information to follow up with them after the interview. I would get their name, e-mail address, mailing address, and phone number if you can. This is critical for you to show them how great you are with following up on the interview. Getting this information gives you a chance to show them you will go the extra mile one last time as well as reminding them who you are.

The third and last question you ask should always be about the interviewer, always! Why you may ask? Very simple answer. You want to get the interviewer talking about him/herself. When people have a chance to talk about themselves, about their career or their accomplishments, it makes them feel good. Remember, this is probably the last thing you do in the interview, so while they are feeling good, because you just gave them a chance to talk about themselves, you leave and they score you. Guess what, your scores go up. Some of you might now believe this can't happen, but let me give you an analogy that might explain how it can work. Suppose you are on the border of an "A" and a "B" in a particular class toward the end of the semester. What do you do? You go visit the professor to ask some questions. By doing this, the professor knows you care. Remember, grades are not all about an exact objective formula. You often have a subjective measure such as class participation that is given to you at the professor's discretion. Interviewers function in a similar way. They are not immune from this, and although no one can guarantee that it will raise your scores, give it a try. You have nothing to lose and everything to gain. **Then of course, the very last thing you do before you walk out is ask for the job!**

[FOLLOWING UP AFTER THE INTERVIEW]

Every book I have read about interviewing tells you to follow up. I am telling you that as well. It is very important. It is often the deciding factor if it is a close decision between candidates. However, many people feel that e-mailing those that interviewed you and thanking them is the best way. It is becoming more and more accepted as the standard thing to do; so you should do it. But the best way to follow up is old school. It is a hand- written thank you note. In the note, you should thank them, of course, but also include one fact from the interview, one specific positive point. The reason you do this is to help them remember you and keep them remembering you. The last thing you should do in the thank you note is to ask for the job. So many times, this step is left out; however, I think it is an effective way of conveying to them that you are serious about their company and want the job. Yes, the assumption is if you are going through all these steps, of course, you want the job. But there were many times in my career, especially when it was a close race between one or more candidates, when someone asked for the job, and that impressed someone enough to bring it up in the debate or argument for them. Plus, often that person got chosen.

> *Even in this day and age of e-mail, hand written "thank you" notes are still very effective and should be part of your follow up process!*

I teach different methods on how to send the thank you note. Regular mail is normally too slow...but it has its place. For example, if you immediately (which means within 12 hours of the interview) e-mail them off a thank you e-mail, you can also follow up with a thank you card by mail. This lets a few days go by in-between your e-mail and when they get the hand written thank you card. This is good because it reminds them of you again and shows that you went one extra step. This is good as we have discussed before because it shows you are willing to go the extra mile, do one more step than most people will do. This is powerful!

Now, you can also send a hand-written note FedEx or UPS overnight.

Again, that shows the extra step, and it will normally get their attention. But the expense is pretty high. Not many college students are willing to shell out $20, probably because if they were anything like me in undergrad, I didn't have an extra $20. Plus, this adds up fast if you have interviewed with several companies.

But I have a solution. After sending the normal thank you e-mail, try this: It is my favorite way of sending a thank you note and what I believe is the most effective hands down. Send the thank you note Priority Mail, but send it in a Priority Mail TUBE. Yes, a tube. Now I expect you have a smile on your face right now. The reason can be answered by this question, 'When was the last time someone sent you something in a tube?' We all get things next day air to us at least from time to time. But when was the last time anyone sent you anything in a tube? When employers get a tube, they immediately are curious. They want to open the tube and see what is in it because no one ever gets a tube. Someone could have a hundred other different types of pieces of mail and I bet you, the first one that gets opened is the tube. It is inexpensive. It is original and different. It will get and keep their attention. It will make you stand out. Plus it shows you are creative and willing to again, go the extra mile and take one more step than most candidates take. It may sound silly, but it really works. Try it.

TECHNICAL INTERVIEWS, SUBJECT MATTER SPECIFIC INTERVIEWS, PANEL INTERVIEWS

For those of you that follow my advice and do remarkably well in the behavioral interviews, sometimes you are left with a final technical or subject matter specific interview. If that is the case, you are really on your own because there is no telling what they are going to ask you. However, there are two things I can share with you to help tremendously in these types of interviews. It uses a manager's number one hiring fear against them and to your advantage. Let me explain. Remember when I told you that the number one fear of hiring managers is to hire someone with a bad attitude who causes problems? Well, this is where you can use that fact to your advantage.

The first question I am usually asked about this type of an interview is: "What you do when you run into a question you can't answer?" Answer: Don't panic. If you really don't know, you should tell them how you would go about finding the answer. Tell them where you would go to find the information. Tell them who you might talk to or what websites you might visit to find the answer. This helps them to understand that if you don't know the answer to something, you will find a way to get the answer. Then, after the interview is done, go find the answer within 24 hours and include it in your thank you card or e-mail. Remember when I was explaining the Behavior section of the interview and I said great candidates go the extra mile or do one step more than most people would do in a similar situation? Well, this does just that. When they receive your thank you card, with the answer to the question you did not know, they will remember you as going the extra mile not that you didn't know the answer. This, most likely, will get you the job, especially when there is close competition. Doing what was just mentioned is exactly what they want to see. This helps convince them you have the right attitude and the "can do" way of thinking. I could argue that this response might be as good or even better than actually knowing the specific answer because no employee will ever know all the answers all the time. However, the real question a recruiter or hiring manager wants to know is what a candidate will do when they don't know the answer. This method of answering a question you don't know speaks volumes to an interviewer. Rarely do candidates understand the power of doing this. Again, it is logical because it addresses the #1 most important attribute companies are looking for, **the right attitude.**

STORY: I was always puzzled by engineering or technical managers that were critical of me not asking enough technical questions to technical candidates. I will take this one step further. There have been plenty of engineering and technical hiring managers that didn't believe in my skills to find great candidates because I couldn't possibly know all the important technical aspects of the jobs they were looking to fill. I almost always won them over by asking them two things: 1. Why do I need to ask technical questions to a technical student who has been at a top university for several years and has a GPA of 3.5? Didn't the school already measure their competence in the chosen field of study over a long period of time? How can my additional technical questions in a 45-minute interview somehow be a better measure? 2. Why don't you choose candidates of your choice and take a few that I recommend and interview them? Then, if my candidates come out on top, we agree to have a new understanding. That new understanding is that you hire the candidates I recommend in the future.

This was a pretty large but strategic risk on my part. I was essentially putting my reputation on the line betting that my candidates would consistently outperform other candidates. But look at the rewards I would have if I won. My candidates would be hired more consistently and faster. I must admit I did not always win. But I win around 9 out of 10 times. That is what built my reputation as a college recruiter. Now the challenge is to keep the quality of the candidates I select consistently very high and to teach others how to do it. Both tasks are very challenging and yet very rewarding. But this is why most companies do behavioral interviews on campus. They are embracing the philosophy of hiring for attitude and training for skill.

Panel interviews always seem to stress college students out more than just a regular one-on-one interview. I can see why. There are more eyes staring at you. More people scoring and evaluating you. Seemingly, more people you need to impress. But for the most part, panel interviews at the college level are no more than just more people asking you the same questions that you would be asked by just one person in a one-on-one interview. I know this because I have led, participated, and organized panel interviews. If there are six questions, panel interviewer number one asks the first question, panel interviewer number two asks the second question, and so on. There is nothing more complicated about it. In addition, there is nothing different you would do in a panel interview than you would in a one-on-one interview except direct your answers to the person asking the question.

Chapter 6

Applying Online

If you don't follow this advice, you probably won't get hired because chances are you won't even be considered. I give you 7 steps to follow that will give you a significant competitive advantage.

In the college recruiting world, it is now being argued that a candidate's ability to strategically navigate the online application process is the most critical part of their job hunt. I am not there yet, but I am starting to lean in that direction because from my experience, there are more people getting hired off the Internet than those through all the college recruiters combined. I see nearly every large, medium, and even small company now having some kind of online employment application process on their website. At Career Fairs and campus events, I consistently and constantly hear company reps instructing candidates to apply online, and that is the only way that they will be considered.

Why do you think the vast majority of companies ask you to go and apply online? If I didn't know and I was reading this, I would probably say something like: "Who cares? Can you just tell me what I have to do to get noticed?" But having a true understanding of why so many companies are adamant about you applying online will help you understand why you have to do it a particular way. After all, you don't want to get lost in the abyss called "Applying Online" like most do right?

There are a few good reasons why companies want you to apply online. The obvious one you already know: it's an efficient way of collecting and tracking a talent pool with little to no touch labor. That saves money. I would agree with this. However, another equally motivating factor for corporate America is FEAR. Fear of litigation and liability. You see, if you are a big company and it can be shown that you didn't treat someone the same as everyone else or you were not fair in the hiring process, you leave yourself open to a potentially very expensive lawsuit. From my experience, that really motivates corporate America. However, if you're a small company, this could potentially cost you your entire business, so no matter what the size of the company, it is important. Now here is the big question: Why is this important for you to know?

The answer is if you understand the motivations behind why companies do it, you are on your way to understanding how you can leverage that to your benefit. Let me explain.

Having some kind of system in place that treats everyone the same and doesn't discriminate among male, female, Black, White, Hispanic, or if your first name is Bill or Saddam, means that no one can be accused of discriminating against a candidate for gender or race or anything else. This reduces liability, which is the goal of corporate America. But there is a down side when the whole system is set up that way, especially at the college level. The problem is how a candidate can differentiate himself/herself when experience levels and degree requirements are

> *Applying online is nothing more than a test of your ability to match the language in your resume with the key words and phrases in the job description you are applying to.*

so similar at hundreds of colleges across the country. For example, let's say you are studying Industrial Engineering (IE), you're a junior and your GPA is a 3.2. How are you supposed to stand out in a pool of one hundred IE's that are juniors with similar GPAs? Sure, we can look at school rankings. But let's say you go to the #10 ranked school for IE, and there are thirty candidates in the pool that go to a less ranked school but have a 3.6 or better. Who should be picked? Who is better?

For an employer, this is a classic case of taking the good with the bad. You don't want to get sued for not treating everyone equally, so you lump everyone together as the same -- until you get to one common point in the process, and this is the key for candidates. That point comes when someone has to get these hundred IEs down to the five they want to interview. How they do that and still treat everyone equally is simple. They just use the computer to search all the resumes for certain key words and phrases that an individual enters in from the job description. It is very similar to a Google search. A person enters in a word or phrase and hits the enter key. If your resume has that key word or phrase, you stay in contention. If not, you are out. Some systems are more sophisticated and give a % compatibility score for the candidate, again just like many search engines. **So creating the Interest Areas section at the bottom of your resume and listing the key words and phrases that you just incorporated into your resume again, gives you a better chance at raising your percentage of compatibility.** This ranks you higher and gives you a better chance at getting considered by the person with hiring authority.

The mistake that the vast majority of college students make when they apply online is they follow the directions blindly without knowing what I have just told you. That is why so many outstanding students complain to me about how they have applied to twenty jobs and never got contacted even once for any of them. I tell them, "Well, you're doing it wrong!" Don't follow the directions? What are you crazy? How are you ever going to get noticed? Remember, they want everyone to do the same things, apply the same way, so everyone is equal, and they can just pick people by a very impersonal process...so no one can yell foul.

[DO IT THIS WAY]

Before you apply to any job opening, before you set up any account or profile on any website, before you do anything, wouldn't it be nice to have the inside story on what the manager is looking for in a candidate? Especially, the required stills or knowledge they want you to have so you can highlight that on your resume? Well, you already have that information in the job description, and here is how you use it and the best way to apply online:

1. Before doing anything else, go to the company website and print out all the jobs that interest you.
2. Take a highlighter and highlight the key words and phrases the manager is using to describe what skills and knowledge they are looking for right from the job description
3. Take the key words and phrases you highlighted and incorporate them throughout your resume.
4. Create a heading on your resume that says, **INTEREST AREAS**, and take all the key words and phrases you highlighted and list them under this heading.
5. Then, set up an account online taking those same key words and phrases and incorporate them into your profile or the "interest areas" section they ask for.
6. THEN, apply to the jobs.
7. As you apply to more openings continually update the key words and phrases in your resume, in your profile or interest area section.

This is called "Reverse Engineering" your resume. From the job description, see what they want first. See what are key words and phrases are that they want to see. Then adjust your resume and apply.

I can't tell you what key words and phrases they are going to use. But let me enlighten you on how this often gets done. You have a person sitting at a computer. Their job is to essentially screen all the resumes that are associated to a particular job. You know what is scary? You would think that these people understand the difference between an Industrial Engineer and Mechanical Engineer or the difference between a Finance major and a Supply Chain Management major. Well, many of them do, but a significant amount may not! Some don't have a clue. Ironically, the same thing as I just told you to do, they do. They just look at the job description and simply look for the key words and phrases the manager put down, type them into a field on the computer, and press enter. Then whoever doesn't have those key words or phrases in their resume, exactly how they typed them in is simply counted out. But be careful. You need to incorporate those key words and phrases verbatim. Remember, you don't know how sophisticated their screening system is. Let me give you an example of a possible scenario of where this comes into play.

There is computer analysis software called Finite Element Analysis, usually used by Mechanical, Aerospace/ Aeronautical, or Civil Engineers to find weak points in a design of some structure. In the engineering community, it is well known as FEA. But here is where the interesting part comes in. So, let's say you are an FEA expert. You have all kinds of experience with it. You teach it to others. You taught advanced classes in FEA to master's candidates in college. You are considered one of the top 10 FEA people in the country. So you find a job opening on a company's website that says they need someone to do FEA full time. This is your perfect job, and you exceed all the qualifications. In the manager's description, they say: "Must be expert at FEA." Now on your resume, you have: "Expert in Finite Element Analysis". Guess what, that person doing the screening may not know that FEA means Finite Element Analysis. So they might just put FEA in the field and press enter. And you know what? You may be counted OUT! Isn't this crazy? Doesn't this shock you? I mean that is not fair! Why should you be counted out just because the person screening the resumes doesn't have a clue?

But now you know. Whether you think that is totally unfair or not, it is a reality in many companies. So use this to your advantage. Outmaneuver the computer screening process so that you have the best chance at being looked at. I am not saying lie or cheat. I am just saying to cater your resume towards those jobs you want the most. Do it this way, and you will have a far better chance at getting to the next step in the process.

When I teach seminars on this topic, some students ask, "Won't they look at my resume and count me out when they see that I just listed all the key words and phrases in the 'Interest Areas' section of my resume?" The answer is they might, especially if you haven't first incorporated those same key words and phrases throughout your resume. That is why doing both is critical. For example, just incorporating the key words and phrases into your resume is great and might get you through to the next step but might not raise your percentage compatibility to a high enough level and you miss the cut off. Remember, at the college level and with the online processes, being the way they are at most companies, there are very few ways for candidates to stand out. There could be ten candidates that by luck score a higher percentage compatibility, and although you meet the all the qualifications, others are more qualified according to the computer, and you are counted out. That is why having the "Interest Areas" section helps. Moreover, if you just cut and paste all the key words in the "Interest Areas" section without also incorporating them into your resume, they will probably see this and count you out.

Lastly, when I say incorporate the key words and phrases into your resume what I mean is to have them distributed throughout your resume. Change or add bullet items in appropriate places. Change your "Objective" to have some in there. The more time you spend on doing it this way, the more calls you are going to get. Try it.

Chapter 7

How to Negotiate Salary

I show you exactly how you do it and teach you a technique that will maximize your chances at getting more money.

A quick note before we get started here. Although this chapter is geared toward those looking for full time, permanent positions as opposed to a co-op or internship, it still has very useful tips and techniques that can help those of you not yet ready for a full time position. Very few companies ever negotiate intern or co-op pay because the number one goal for the student is to gain experience, and the number one goal for the company is to evaluate intern and co-op candidates while giving them some experience. Money is important but not as important as the experience. Also, these same basic negotiating techniques can be used for many situations. For example: I have used and taught friends and interns how to use them to negotiate the price of a new car. It really works!

There is a book out there called *Knock'em Dead* by Martin Yate. It was originally recommended to me by my brother-in-law many years ago. It is especially good when you have a few years of experience under your belt. I believe it is still one of the best books out there for preparing experienced people for the job search. I especially like the chapter on salary negotiation. I know some of Mr. Yates' suggestions helped me at different times along my career, and that is why you may see some similarities. What I have tried to do is take what I have learned over the years, along with some of his suggestions that have helped me, and come up with a simple method of negotiating salary for those just coming out of college.

Salary negotiation is said to be an art form. There are entire books dedicated to negotiating one thing or another including your pay. From my experience, about two thirds of college candidates fail to even try to negotiate their starting salary; and the one third that does, doesn't really know how to do it.

Did you know that failing to negotiate your starting salary at your first job by just $2000 will cost you about $250,000 over a career! That is called, "Time Value of Money", and those MBAs that are reading know exactly what I'm talking about. That is an awfully large amount of money to leave on the table.

As I stated, only about one third of the college candidates try to negotiate their starting salary. Surprisingly, those that do try are often successful. So, if there is one point I want to make in this chapter, it is to **TRY!**

Those people who fail to negotiate are just very uncomfortable and/or scared. Some think if they do, they'll blow it, and the company will take back the offer leaving them with nothing. Others are scared that they will sound too greedy. Still others are scared that it won't work, and they will fail. However, most candidates are scared because they simply don't know how to do it.

Negotiating at this level is really not that complex. It really boils down to two things (1.) being realistic about the range of salary in your field (2.) Asking for it in a way that is courteous, respectful, and yet very effective.

STEP #1: Learning how to negotiate your salary is all about data, research, and preparation. It is about you taking some time to investigate what I like to call the Salary Market Range (SMR). The SMR is nothing more than getting on the Internet and finding out what new college grads in your major are getting. You are interested in the low and high salary range. This is the base information you need. Then, if you can get actual salary numbers from your school in your major, that is even better because it more closely reflects what your market value is. The bottom line here is that you have to define for yourself a low and high number for your salary range. The difference between these numbers needs to be realistic; I would say about five to six thousand dollars.

STEP #2: Put together a one-page report. In the report you should have the data you found from your research that supports the salary range you are asking for. (Entitle it "Executive Briefing: Salary Market Range for 'enter your name'". Organize the data in a way that is direct and to the point. Site those websites and sources where you got your information. Include any charts or graphs that help your cause. No more than one page! Then, at the bottom, the last statement should be: "Conclusion: Appropriate salary range $54,000-$59,000." Then run it by the people at your Career Center to get a realistic perspective of the range and a final check.

I know many of you will not take the time to do this step. Again, I am realistic when I teach and from my experience some will take the time to do it and some will not. But the importance of this step is twofold. First, by going through this process, it teaches and confirms what salary range is realistic and appropriate for you. This provides the extra confidence some may need to believe that they are worth what they are asking for, and it will motivate them to actually ask when they normally would not have. Second, it gives you a document you can e-mail or fax over to the person you're negotiating with to help motivate them to increase your salary. Even if they have other data that might dispute yours, even if they don't agree with your data, that is not the point! The point of you sending it over to them is to show them you did your homework, that you are prepared, that you are taking this seriously, and that you're willing to go the extra mile. But, above all, it shows them that they will be getting an

> *They key to find out what salary range is right for you, starts with research. If you don't know where to begin, go visit your career center.*

employee with all these great attributes if they just come up a little on the salary range. Ding, Ding, Ding, Ding! The sound of more money!

Once you have your range and your Executive Briefing, now you are ready to go to the next step, which is how to ask for more money. I am going to give you a simple and effective way that you can remember even under pressure. From my experience, I know many are just uncomfortable with this process. Some so uncomfortable that you just won't do it. Others are so nervous or just stressed out over this; again, they won't even attempt it. Even if you're not too stressed, you need a good technique and method that will work for anyone you are negotiating with. In reality, it is not always your direct manager or even anyone in your chain of command that you may be negotiating with. But you are not in control of who you will be negotiating with, so you need one way that will work most of the time with most people. It needs to be simple and not complicated so under pressure you don't forget. Similar to my philosophy on interviewing, you need a process or method that will help you even if the person negotiating with you is not a good negotiator.

The first thing you do when getting an offer is to say "Thank You". The key is to be nice, be gracious, and respectful no matter what; even if the one you're negotiating with is not. You never know who is having a bad day. You never know the motivations of the other person.

STORY: I have seen people negotiate with potential new college hires who just sound irritated and angry when someone tries to negotiate their salary. Later I have learned and overheard them explain their frustration by saying things like, "I have been in the company for ten years, and I don't even make that much!" "It is not right for a new college grad to make more than me to begin with, and then they ask for more." I have also heard people say comments like, "My son or daughter didn't get nearly that much out of college…What makes them think they are so much better and worth more?" For the most part, those that negotiate with you are professionals. But those are not the ones you have to worry about.

This is why being nice, respectful, and non-confrontational is so important. You never know who you are going to be negotiating with, and you never know their personal feelings or motivations. I give you this example again to educate you to prepare for the most difficult situation and, therefore, you will be prepared for any situation.

Negotiating is a lot of psychology, and I could give you all the in-depth psychological reasons why something works, but you might fall asleep so just remember this: The language you use needs to be nice, never confrontational, and never even approaching an ultimatum. Calm, cool, and collected at all times. And always start out by saying, "Thank you for the offer," no matter what the offer is. The reason you do this is to put them in a positive mind set.

Since you have your low and high numbers that make up your range and these numbers are backed up by research and data, you now know what to ask for. Now if they (when I say they I mean a company representative) come up with a number first, then you simply state your range, never just a number. To give you an example: let's say after you did your research, your range is $54,000-$59,000. They offer you $51,000. You counter offer this way: **First, thank you for the offer. We are close! My ideal salary for this position is fifty-nine thousand with my range being between fifty-four and fifty-nine thousand.** That's it! That is all you have to do at least initially. This will often motivate them to bump you up, and at the very least, put you in a position to be considered for more. Remember, it has been my experience that two thirds of candidates at the college level don't even try to negotiate.

What if they want you to come up with a number first? Well, this is simple. Since you did the research, you just state the same thing: "First, thank you for the offer. My ideal salary for this position is fifty-nine thousand with my range being between fifty-four and fifty-nine thousand."

What if they give you an offer that is really low, but you really want to work for that company in that job. For example, let's say your range is the same as above, and they offer you $45,000. Really, nothing changes here. Remember, this could be a tactic or just a method they use to start low in hopes to get you for less money...because again, they know most don't negotiate. Don't worry about that. You just say the same thing: "First, thank you for the offer. We are close! My ideal salary for this position is fifty-nine thousand with my range being between fifty four-and fifty-nine thousand." Yes, I know they are not close! So why should you say, "We are close?" But that is not the point. You tell them, "We are close," to keep them in a positive mindset, to keep them on your side.

Now, what if they offer you more than your salary range? That is great! And you know what you should do? Ask for more! How you do that is what I like to refer to as the two-five rule. To explain how the two-five rule works, let's continue on with our example range from above $54,000-$59,000. They give you an offer of $61,000 before you even get a chance to state your range. Well, you add $2000 on to the $61,000 (which makes your bottom range at $63,000), and then you add $5000 on to that (which makes your upper range of $68,000.) Yes, this is a little simple math. But under stress, I have seen people with master's degrees in engineering unable to do the math on the spot under pressure. That is why I have made it simple. The two-five rule. Again, if the initial offer comes in over your range, you add $2000 on to their offer, and that is your low range number. Then you add $5000 on to that and that is your upper range number. Then you say, "First, thank you for the offer. We are close! My ideal salary for this position is sixty eight thousand with my range being between sixty-three and sixty-eight thousand."

See? It's just that easy. Now I realize that if the initial offer is higher than your range to begin with, then the Executive Briefing you created won't work in its present format. But isn't that a nice position to be in?

There are dozens and dozens of questions I am asked after presenting this information. The reason is most candidates want the answers to any and all situations that could come up. I can't answer them all, but let me answer a few that come up on a regular basis.

Question: What if after doing everything you said, they just say no?

Answer: Rarely does this actually happen but it does happen. Usually, they say something like, "This is what we start off our college grads at." So what you should do in this case is take them off the subject. Ask about benefits. Ask about the corporate culture. Ask about the surrounding area. Ask about what else is included in the offer. Then, after they talk about that for a while, say, "This sounds like a great opportunity and thank you for explaining the details to me. We are close. If we just could move a little on the salary range. My ideal salary for this position is fifty-nine thousand with my range being between fifty-four and fifty-nine thousand." That sometimes works.

Question: What if they still don't come up?

Answer: Then you have a decision to make. If you really like the job and really like the company, take the position. Some companies just can't or won't give you more money. However, your job was to ask in a way that gave you the best chance at getting more. You did that.

Question: What about in bad economic times? Does your approach change?

Answer: No, not really. If a company is hiring, even in bad economic times, they still want the best. You should still ask the same way but understand that they may be a little less flexible because they have a lot more candidates to pick from.

Question: What about cost of living?

Answer: Before you get into this argument, you must first evaluate the offer as a whole. For example, companies are aware of the cost of living in different areas. They have to be because if their offers are too low, no one will come to work for them there. But what if a company is willing to pay 100% of your master's degree, but their offer is $10,000 less than another company that will give you nothing towards your education? Well, a good graduate school can be upwards of $20,000 per year. So who really has the better offer? Or look at the benefits package. What if a company gives you $5000 less a year, but you have excellent medical and dental with low or no deductibles? The other company is offering only major medical coverage and all the other expenses come out of your pocket? The point I am making is be smart enough to not just jump at the money. Take a look at the value of the whole offer. What you will normally find is that the company that you really want for might have a lower offer, but it still might be the best offer.

STORY: Back in the day, not too long ago, I remember coming out of college and scoring an interview with a company for a coveted rotational program. It was extremely competitive, and I was told later that out of the best candidates they could find at one hundred and thirty six schools, they only selected 11 for interviews and took the top 6 for the job. I was lucky enough to be chosen as one of those six. I remember when my offer came to me. I remember feeling good that I got it but a little let down over the salary. But the offer as a whole was an excellent one, but I still wanted to try to see if I could get a little more money. So, like most, I really didn't know how to go about it. I did do the research to find information that would support my asking for more money and put a report together. Knowing what I know now, I did a lot of things that were wrong in the negotiation. However, I did ask, and I did have back-up data. And you know what? They gave more. I didn't know at the time that it was, at least in their eyes, a lot more until I arrived for my first day. I remember going into Human Resources (HR) with a few of the other candidates that got hired in. The HR person did her thing with us: filling out paper work and then entering it into the computer. I was so excited. However, when the HR person got to me, she started to enter all the information in and had to stop and call a supervisor over. They started to discuss something and then both got irritated. While one of them was doing something on another computer, I was enthusiastically asking a few questions. But the tone and attitude of the HR person had changed. She seemed irritated with me and gave me very short answers. I later found out that because I had negotiated so well, they had to go into their system and over-ride some things to get my salary up to what I was offered. They were not happy because it made more work for them. But I was.

The most important thing about negotiating salary? **TRY!** You will probably be surprised by the success you will have and how easy it was getting that success.

Chapter 8

Working With Your Career Center

How to do it and what you really can get out of it. This is more important than you might think.

Guilty as charged! Like so many students I have met over the years, I, too, had a big misconception about my career center when I was a student. I admit, I went in there once and never went back because I thought I was being treated like everyone else. I didn't feel as if they understood my needs or what I wanted. I felt they basically just told me the same thing they tell everyone that comes in the door. And I was right! They did! But there is a lot more to the story.

> ***The single biggest mistake a student can make in their job search is to not include their career center as part of their overall strategy!***

Let me put this as clearly as I can. The career center is a powerful tool in your job search. It should not be your only tool, but it should be one of your primary ones.

Those working at your career center have to use what I call the "shotgun approach." There are so many students that want and need help, they must, at least initially, adopt an approach that gives everyone the basics. It is logical. It makes sense because they need to try to help hundreds and even thousands of students. So, if you feel you are not getting the personal attention you need, then it is your responsibility to change it. If you take the time to get to know your career counselor by name, and if you meet with them one-on-one enough times so they know your name and say hello when they pass you on campus, that is when you will start to see the greatness of the career center. There is no way each counselor has the time to come up with an individual career plan for every student at the school. It is impossible. There isn't enough time in the day. So you want to know who they help? They help those that take the time to get to know them. Those that show them, over time, that they are serious about wanting their help. Those that meet with them consistently, take their advice, and take the time to follow their advice and follow through. If you do this, you will have a distinct advantage over most all other students when it comes to finding and landing the job you want.

Oftentimes, the career counselors have to evaluate whether or not they should give a student more time. Because of the limited time they have with any one individual student, why should they invest their time in helping a student who doesn't follow through or who has a bad attitude with them? They need to concentrate on the students with the right attitudes. Sound familiar? It should. It is the same basic philosophy as a college recruiter; attitude is everything. They give the time to those students with the right attitudes.

Students don't realize just how powerful their college career center staff is. They have direct lines to all recruiters. They know what companies are looking for in candidates so they can help students cater their approaches to get the positive results they are looking for. **Bottom Line: Go to your career center and try my approach. It will be well worth your time.**

Last, you want to know a great way to fully take advantage of all the great information the career center has to offer? Work or volunteer there. I can't express to you how incredibly effective this is for you getting all the great advice and inside information.

STORY: Over the years I have interviewed and evaluated thousands of students. One observation that I have made is those that have taken advantage of what the career center has to offer as well as those that have done at least one co-op or internship are far more prepared, get far more interview invitations, score significantly higher in interviews, and get more job offers.

Those at the career center from the university I graduated from know me well. We have been working together for over ten years now, and I really have developed some close professional relationships with those in the office. I have really come to learn how incredibly talented they are and how sincere they are in wanting to help students put their best foot forward. However, even though I graduated from there with two degrees, a BS and MS, and even though my current company is one of if not their top employer of their students, and even though we have been working together for over a decade, two things I wish were changed. The first thing is that there still is no required course all students must take before they graduate that teaches them the best ways to prepare for the job search. The other is there is still no mandatory co-op/internship requirement to graduate.

Recently I have inquired with the career center to see how I might work with them to get these ideas implemented. I sincerely believe these are the two things that will help the students and the school the most. It really seems logical to me, especially taking into consideration what I have seen and experienced. The better, more prepared students are when dealing with potential employers and the job search process, the more get hired, the more money they make, and the better the reputation of the school becomes over time.

I still don't understand why students and parents would pay tens of thousands of dollars to go to college each year, and yet the college does not require them to take a class on how to prepare for getting a job and how to find a job. Nor do I understand how students, who don't get an internship or co-op with a company while they are going to college, can think they can compete with students that have that experience. The point of this story to you is: get yourself down to your career center ASAP! The advice, skills, and knowledge provided by the counselors may give you the competitive edge needed to land the full time job or co-op/internship you really want. The career center is a great place to learn more about co-op/internships and put yourself on a path to getting one before you graduate! Do yourself a favor: no matter what year you are in college get down to your career center ASAP!

Chapter 9

Miscellaneous & Rapid Fire Advice

Assorted advice to help you put your best foot forward. Also included is specific advice for each year of college.

- Keep your grades up as high as you can: Grades aren't everything but when there are a number of candidates for a particular job, it is the easiest way a hiring manager to count you out.

- Being involved in outside clubs, groups, and activities is important but not at the expense of good grades. If you are involved with a lot of things outside the classroom and your grades are lower because of it, stop some or even all of those things to bring your grades up.

- Get at least one summer internship or co-op in your field of study, before you graduate undergrad. The more, the better. In general, you will have a very hard time competing against those students that have this experience if you don't. It could mean the difference of you getting the job or not getting the job. It is that important. Some colleges, like Rochester Institute of Technology (RIT), require up to 5 quarters of co-op, in some degree programs, in order to graduate. From my experience, this gives their students a HUGE competitive advantage. RIT students are consistently some of the best-prepared candidates to enter the job force full time.

- Transferable skills: Whatever internship, co-op, or part time campus job you might take, the best ones are those with direct transferable skills. To explain what I mean by direct transferable skills here is an example: If your major is accounting, the work experience companies most like to see is accounting experience. Being a waiter or waitress makes money and you get some good experience working with people, but it doesn't hold the same value.

- Get a copy of your past performance evaluations. Use them in your job search, especially if you do an internship or co-op. Remember, people that hire college candidates want to do what they can to reduce their risk of hiring a bad candidate. Having past performance evaluations helps alleviate this risk in their minds.

- Get leadership experience. Become an officer in a student group you are in. Offer to be the team leader in your class assignments that involve a group project. Not only will it help you answer interview questions from a leadership perspective, it also displays the leadership attribute that recruiters and those with hiring authority look for.

- **Freshmen:** Your number one goal is to keep your grades as high as they can be. Then have a plan to get some intern or co-op experience as soon as you can. When it comes to internships or co-ops, companies usually like to concentrate on upper-classman first because they have more core classes completed, and they can be given higher-level tasks. That is not to say as a Freshman you should not try or apply. The opposite is true. Go up to the booths at the career fairs. Introduce yourself. Let them know you are a freshman and ask them this: "What are the things you look for in a candidate when considering them for an intern or co-op?" Tell them that you came to introduce yourself in hopes that you could get some information on the best ways to get an internship or co-op with their company. Remember, you want them to remember you, so if you don't get an internship or co-op your first year, they are at least familiar with you next year. Plus, apply online; you might get lucky.

- **Sophomores:** Although you are still a little early for some companies, you should be hitting the career fairs and practicing your approach, focusing your attention on getting a co-op or internship. To stand out, you may want to list the upper level courses in the major you are taking or have taken. Of course, you should be aggressively applying online to any internship or co-op that is directly applicable to your major. You should go find your career counselor at your career center and start your professional relationship with them.

- **Juniors:** You are an upper classman, and that is what most companies want to concentrate on when looking for interns or co-ops. The reason for this is that most Juniors have committed to their major and the statistics suggest that once a student gets to "Junior" status, they have settled on a major and are unlikely to change it. This is important to companies because the odds are the experience they provide you in your particular major will benefit them if they hire you when you graduate. Apply like mad to websites for all co-op or internship positions you are interested in. Your resume should be solid. Your approach should be solid. If you have not yet been to your career center and know who your career counselor is, you are behind schedule. You should have your stories to answer interview questions ready to go and should be practicing them.

- **Seniors & Super Seniors:** You should have it all together. Your resume, your stories to answer interview questions, everything. You should be on a first name basis with your career counselor at your career center. You should have a copy **of your past performance evaluations already in your career** portfolio ready to show anyone that is interested in seeing your resume. Remember, statistically the company where you do your last internship or co-op is most likely where you are going to work full time **if** you exceed expectations. To put it another way, the easiest way to get a full time offer with a company you want to work for full-time in the future is to co-op or intern with them. Some of you may have one summer left that you can do an internship; others may just be looking for a full-time job. Either way, you need your approach to be smooth and polished. And, of course, you should apply online and apply often.

- **Graduate Students:** Your approach should be similar to what Seniors do, so please read above. There seems to be a misconception out there that graduate students can't or shouldn't intern. That is just wrong. As a matter of fact, everything is sped up. In your first year of graduate school, you could do a summer internship. Then as soon as that is done, you are in your full-time job search mode. Companies expect you to have excellent stories to answer interview questions with because you have more experience to draw from.

- **Ph.D. Students:** You can intern or co-op as well, but usually your academic schedule along with your research and dissertation work limits you. What you need to concentrate on is finding companies that have exactly what you want to do. I often ask Ph.D. students to explain their dissertation research to me in only a few sentences, and then explain how their expertise in their selected field can directly transfer to what my company does. You need to be able to do this. This is the most common mistake I see from candidates at this level. Essentially, you have not worked on how to sell yourself to a company. Get good at doing that, and more companies will be interested.

- **E-mail Me:** Mark@DoThisGetHired.com and let me know about your successes with this information. Please feel free to e-mail with any feedback or questions you might have. If you want to learn more, please visit my website at www.DoThisGetHired.com and check out the great information there.

Made in the USA
Charleston, SC
18 August 2010